A WALK THROUGH
ANCIENT ROME

Also by Philip Matyszak and published
by Michael O'Mara Books:

24 Hours in Ancient Rome
24 Hours in Ancient Athens
A Year in the Life of Ancient Greece

A WALK THROUGH
ANCIENT ROME

A TOUR OF THE HISTORICAL SITES
THAT SHAPED THE CITY

PHILIP
MATYSZAK

Michael O'Mara Books Limited

First published in Great Britain in 2024 by
Michael O'Mara Books Limited
9 Lion Yard
Tremadoc Road
London SW4 7NQ

Copyright © Philip Matyszak 2024

A CIP catalogue record for this book is available from the British Library.

Papers used by Michael O'Mara Books Limited are natural, recyclable products
made from wood grown in sustainable forests. The manufacturing processes
conform to the environmental regulations of the country of origin.

ISBN: 978-1-78929-522-1 in hardback print format
ISBN: 978-1-78929-523-8 in ebook format

1 2 3 4 5 6 7 8 9 10

Cover design by Ana Bjezancevic
Cover illustrations by Victor McLindon
Photographs of *Plastico di Roma Imperiale* by Adrian Goldsworthy
Internal illustrations by Peter Liddiard
Some line illustrations based on Rich's Dictionary
Designed and typeset by Design23

Printed and bound by CPI Group (UK) Ltd, Croydon, CRO 4YY

www.mombooks.com

CONTENTS

PREFACE

The city of Rome and the Roman Empire had two very different destinies from the second century AD onwards. While the empire peaked under the Antonine emperors (AD 98–180) and spiralled down thereafter, the city of Rome grew ever larger and more opulent until the fifth century when the empire's collapse made the city an irresistible target for barbarian pillagers.

In the late fourth century, Rome could claim to be the greatest city in the world, in population, historical significance and architectural heritage. This, then, is a walk to be taken through the city in the sunset – for Rome itself was never grander or more magnificent than just before it fell.

The book is written as a set of walks through Rome because most Romans walked. It was possible to travel in a litter carried by bearers, but only the most aristocratic of ladies did this – not least because the thronged streets made this form of transport somewhat slower than going on foot. There are eleven walks in all, based very roughly on the fourteen Augustan administrative districts of Rome. They will certainly take in the grand monuments such as the unforgettable Colosseum and the imperial palaces, but the intention is to step beyond that to give a flavour of the city as a whole.

As well as maps showing how your walk will proceed through the ancient city, line drawings show an artist's reconstruction of some of the places and people you would see. For these walks will not just take us through the city, but also back to a different time when Rome was at the peak of its majesty. Therefore, in this walk we shall not see the – sometimes frankly pathetic – modern remnants of once-great buildings and monuments. Instead, we shall see them in their glory, as their designers intended them to be seen fifteen hundred or more years ago. So, with each of the walks described here, you must move your consciousness back through the centuries so that you walk the streets of ancient Rome and mingle with the Romans of the late fourth century AD.

There was a huge disparity in wealth between the few who lived in those luxurious edifices usually described in textbooks as the 'typical Roman home' and those who lived in actual Roman homes – crammed five to a room in bustling apartment buildings. Romans could live like that because their culture had a huge tolerance for crowding, and because life was mainly lived outdoors and in company. Defecation, like dining, was a social occasion and many Romans were never alone from the moment they were born (surrounded by relatives) until the moment they died (surrounded by a different generation of relatives).

One consequence of this was that Rome's population took up a smaller portion of the city than might be expected. Much of the remaining area was taken up by gardens and monumental or administrative spaces, almost all of which were open to the public. Romans might have lacked elbow room but they did not lack for entertainment, with many busy, well-stocked markets and places around them to relax and exercise in. We shall visit them in all these places.

This walk takes us through almost a thousand years of Rome as a city, from the Hut of Romulus to the Arch of Constantine. The ghosts of Trajan, Nero and Cicero walk with us, for we shall stand where they stood and see the same things they have seen. (And so much more ... the Rome of Maxentius in AD 312 would have impressed the socks off Cicero who lived in the more basic city of three centuries before.) Likewise, where contemporary Romans have discussed their city, their voices are brought into the conversation, whether it is the satirist Martial cursing the muddy streets or the later poet Claudian lauding the majesty of the Capitol.

While the walk describes what a tourist would experience walking the streets of fifth-century Rome, this book is for readers sitting in a twenty-first century armchair. Therefore, dates have been converted from the Roman AUC (*ab urbe condita* – 'from the foundation of the city') to the more conventional AD and BC. Measurements have been given in general terms where possible ('five minutes' walk', 'a hand span', etc.), but where more precise figures are required these are given in modern metric rather than in *stades* or cubits. Each chapter ends with a summary called 'The Twenty-First Century Walk' where we retrace the steps taken fifteen centuries ago and see what has become of the urban environment and its monuments in the meantime.

We start south of Rome in the Alban Hills, where our walks and the history of Rome both begin. That smoky smudge on the horizon is the great sprawling city itself – let's go get it!

EXTRA MUROS: FROM THE ALBAN HILLS TO ROME

In the Footsteps of Romulus and Remus

Rome is a city rich in history and legend. In fact, many of the legends of Rome start before the city itself began. So, it is appropriate that we start our first walk in the Alban Hills near the city where Rome's founders Romulus and Remus were born. The city of Alba Longa gets its name because it was stretched out along a ridge overlooking the blue waters of the Alban Lake. The legendary city's history goes back centuries, for we are told that it was founded around 1151 BC. The founder was Ascanius, the son of the Trojan hero Aeneas. Ascanius, also known as Iulus, is the alleged father of the Julian line of the Caesars of Rome.

> *Alba [Longa] occupied the area between a mountain and a lake and these natural defences made the city as hard to capture as if it were surrounded by walls. For the mountain is both rugged and high and the lake is expansive and deep. The locals can conserve the waters as they wish, releasing them through sluices to the plain below. There is a marvellous view of these plains, the fecundity of which produces fruit of a variety to match anywhere else in Italy. Also there is the exceptional wine that they call 'Alban'. Apart from Falernian, it is superior to all others.*
>
> Dionysius of Halicarnassus, *Roman Antiquities* (1.66)

Now to begin the long walk to Rome. This walk is twelve miles long (just short of 20 kilometres), so it is best to start early. In an era where

Lost City or Myth?

Alba Longa was considered the dominant city of Latium in the centuries before Rome's founding. Later, the city was captured after a struggle with its upstart colony and rival, the city of Rome. Thereafter, Alba was destroyed by the conquerors and the people of the city added to the growing population of Rome.

Sceptics may doubt the existence of this ancient city, for as with many of the legends of early Rome, physical evidence is scant. Nevertheless, even now the rites allegedly established by the kings of Alba Longa continue to be celebrated on Mount Alba. Every year the consuls of Rome gather with delegates of the Latin tribes to celebrate the festival of the Feriae Latinae. Each delegate brings offerings of a rustic type suitable to the antiquity of the proceedings. Cheeses, wholegrain breads and fresh fruits are consumed along with the meat of a white heifer sacrificed for the occasion.

walking is the main means of travel, twelve miles is something of a stroll for the locals. Horse-drawn vehicles are relatively expensive and many pedestrians make a daily commute of twelve miles or more to the city and back, grateful for the cool, mosquito-free air for which the Alban Hills are famed. In fact, a look across the Alban Hills will show that the slopes are studded with the villas of the very wealthy who come here to escape the noise and heat of the city. (It's never hard to locate Rome, just look to the north for the column of smoke rising from thousands of cooking fires, bakeries and smithies for some idea of what the locals are getting away from.)

A villa in these hills is a much-vaunted sign of wealth and prestige, while Alban farms have long been the playthings of multi-millionaires wanting to show off their rustic roots. Sadly, you would have to go in the opposite direction to see one of the most spectacular sights of the Alban Hills. This is the summer retreat of the Emperor Caligula, built upon the shores of Lake Nemi, the waters of which are so spectacularly clear that they are called the 'Mirror of Diana' – the Diana in question being the Roman goddess of nature and the wilderness.

Caligula maintained two luxury pleasure barges on the lake – sumptuously decadent vessels over 200 feet long, stationed not far from the temple of the goddess, which is itself believed to be the richest in Italy. The priest of this temple is a runaway slave, who by tradition keeps his post until he is slain in combat with his successor – another runaway slave. Also here is the small town of Aricia, where the mother of the Emperor Augustus was born.

As you might expect given the wealth and pedigree of the denizens of the Alban Hills, the road to Rome is in superb condition and were it not for the constant traffic of horses and ox-carts, walking along it would be a pleasure. (Fortunately, most riders stay on the soft shoulders of the road to spare the unshod hooves of their horses.) The road itself is surfaced with smooth volcanic rock with concrete between the slabs, making the road so smooth that one cannot feel the joints. Because of this, even walking barefoot and blindfolded one would know this is the oldest and best-maintained of all Roman roads, the famous Via Appia.

By this point in the walk, tombs line the roadside, for it is forbidden to bury the dead within Rome, and burials along the roads leading from the city make it easier to visit the graves of one's ancestors. There is no *memento mori*, however, for the more than 6,000 people who died along this road in 71 BC. These were rebel slaves in the army of Spartacus, captured after the defeat of their leader. The Roman general Marcus Licinius Crassus had these men crucified along the Appian Way, so that their tortured deaths would serve as a grim warning to anyone else contemplating a challenge to the power of Rome.

The Appian Way

The Via Appia was built in 312 BC with pedestrians in mind, although admittedly the sort of pedestrians who wear heavy armour and carry swords and shields. At the time of construction, the Romans were fighting the warlike Sabine tribe for control of the wealthy plain of Campania, and the city needed a road that could move troops speedily to the battlefield. As a result, the Via Appia cuts through the countryside as straight as an arrow. The stretch of the Appian Way between Alba Longa and Rome is known as the Via Norba because it runs through the Alban Hills to the town of Norba, which overlooks the Pontine marshes (and goes on to the city of Terracina beyond).

These days the only soldiers on the road are those proceeding to distant parts of the empire, for the Emperor Trajan built an extension taking the road as far as the heel of Italy. Bitter experience and the loss of tens of thousands of men at sea has taught the Romans not to trust their armies to Neptune, so troops on the move embark not at the nearby Ostia or Puetoli, but at Brundisium, where one can hope for good weather for the few hours it takes to cross the Adriatic Sea to Greece.

The Tomb of Caecilia Metella

As we approach within three miles of the city, the tombs get ever larger and more impressive. Most impressive of all is the Tomb of Caecilia. Crassus was brutal enough to leave thousands of corpses rotting at the roadside, but his son decided that on this same road only the grandest of tombs would do for his wife, one Caecilia Metella. Indeed, apart from the particularly exuberant efforts of a few emperors (which we shall come to later), few tombs are as impressive as this. So large is this mausoleum that it might be mistaken for a small castle – as it will indeed become in later ages.

The base is a large raised square standing over 8 metres tall. It

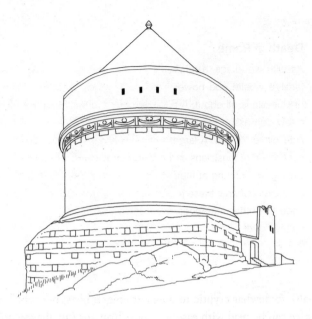

is faced with travertine stone, but the interior is filled mainly with layers of solid Roman concrete. This base is large enough for peasants of later times to grow a grain crop out of the reach of predators, while the concrete itself is a marvel of technology. The concrete contains crystals that dissolve on contact with water and then harden afterwards, leaving the concrete stronger than before, while the crack through which the water entered is sealed in the process. Vitruvius presciently remarked that the use of such concrete results in structures that 'endure through the ages without falling into ruin'.

From the huge plinth that constitutes the base of the tomb rises a rotunda towering 11 metres and giving the entire structure a height of almost 22 metres. The travertine rock facing is decorated with friezes showing garlands, fruit and ox skulls (this is a tomb, after all). Passers-by are informed by a large inscription that this monument is for *CAECILIAE Q CRETICI F METELLAE CRASSI* (to Caecilia Metella, daughter of Quintus Creticus and wife of Crassus). Roman tombstones have a number of conventional abbreviations, which are

Death in Rome

As with weddings, a funeral is an opportunity to display the family's wealth and power, which is basically what the Tomb of Caecilia is all about. A poor person's funeral will have only a few depressed family members preceded by the bier and a flute player or two. A larger funeral is a noisy affair with a full contingent of musicians and a horde of semi-hysterical women wailing and tearing at their clothes and hair. The torn clothing is an expense that these professional mourners add to their bill once the other attendees have departed, suitably impressed by their grief.

initially somewhat cryptic to amateur epigraphists, but which with practice can be read with ease – as most Romans can already do.

While no other tomb along the road is quite as grand as that for Caecilia Metella, the nearer one gets to Rome the more thickly these tombs cluster by the roadside. Do not be surprised if your approach to Rome is interrupted by the need to stand aside as yet another funeral procession goes by. Roman burials are a serious business, not least because a family member who is not interred with the proper rites and due ceremony might hang around their former home as a thoroughly disgruntled spirit.

If you have to stand aside for one of these events, look to your right. There, across the flat and fertile fields, you will see what appears to be a long grey wall stretching across the horizon as far as the eye can see. That's one of Rome's famous aqueducts – well, actually two of them, because at this point the Aqua Tepula, built in 126 BC, has joined the Aqua Marcia. Between them these aqueducts bring tens of thousands of gallons of water to Rome every day. Much of this journey to the city is through underground channels. However, before it enters Rome the water is kept at a higher level by concrete-lined channels atop a series of massive arches. When the water does eventually descend to ground level within the walls of Rome, its own weight combines with gravity to power the various fountains that dot the city.

The Grotto of Egeria

By now Rome is right ahead with the Porta Appia, your entry point through the walls, within sight. Before you plunge into Rome proper, this would be a good moment to take a break in a pleasant grotto that lies between the Appian Way and the Via Latina, which also approaches Rome from the south. (Had you taken the Via Latina you would also have had a chance to visit the tombs of the deceased, for beside this road are found the vast and growing catacombs where the Christians of Rome inter their dead. Etymologists might also like to take a look at the nearby quarry, which is the namesake of these burial tunnels: 'catacomb' translates roughly as 'beside the quarry'.)

Peaceful though the grotto may be, it is also in a way a burial site and a very ancient one at that. Rome's second king was Numa Pompilius. Unlike the warlike Romulus, Numa was mainly interested in putting the infant state of Rome on a sound footing with the appropriate laws and religious observances. In this, Numa had the very competent assistance of the water nymph Egeria (who also hails from the Alban Hills). The Romans are uncertain how closely the king and nymph worked together and whether this relationship

was purely legalistic – in part because Numa himself was apparently rather close-mouthed on the topic.

However, one rather clear hint comes from the fact that when Numa passed away (peacefully and from old age – an exceptional feat for a Roman king), Egeria literally dissolved into tears of sorrow.

> *Nymphs of the grove and lake entreated her to cease her lamentation and offered her words of consolation … yet this could not ease the grief of sorrowful Egeria. She laid herself down … given over to tears until her faithful mourning moved* [the goddess] *Diana to pity. She changed Egeria's body to a spring, and her limbs formed a clear-flowing stream.*

> Ovid, *Metamorphoses* (457 & passim)

That's the spring in the grotto beside the Porta Appia. These days the quiet rural spot has been embellished (or 'ruined' according to the poet Juvenal in his third Satire) by a marble nymphaeum. If you arrive early enough in the day, you'll encounter one of the Vestal Virgins, come from her shrine to collect water. The water in the Vestal shrine comes solely from this spring, which is for the use of the Vestals alone.

Those refreshed by a moment of quiet repose in the grotto of Egeria might find they have the energy for one final stop before entering the city. It's another tomb, naturally, but much more besides. It was built by the Emperor Maxentius and the family mausoleum is part of a larger complex that includes a luxurious villa and the second-largest chariot racetrack in the environs of the city. (The largest one is of course the appropriately named Circus Maximus, situated smack in the middle of Rome.)

After the death of Maxentius, the Emperor Constantine took over the site, but like many of the monuments along this stretch of road, Maxentius' villa and racetrack are in some disrepair and slowly falling towards ruin.

After leaving Maxentius behind and rejoining the traffic on the Via Appia there may be some delay, for traffic entering and leaving the city must pass through the bottleneck of the gate itself. Two hundred years ago, this problem did not exist. Traffic rolled and strolled unhindered down the Via Appia as far as the Porta Capena, just over three-quarters of a Roman mile down the road.

Those were the days when the power of Rome was undisputed all over Italy and far beyond, and no one had threatened the city of Rome itself since Hannibal in the days of the Roman Republic. Like the Spartans before them, the Romans of the early empire took pride in the fact that their city was defended by its soldiers rather than by its walls. This pride has taken something of a dent since, with massive barbarian raids penetrating deep into Italy, and these days even mighty Rome is no longer as secure as it once was. In the year AD 270, the Emperor Aurelian (perhaps the most underrated of all emperors) decided that Rome needed the protection of an extra wall.

Rome did indeed already have a city wall – and this wall is largely standing. However, the extent to which the city had outgrown those defences can be guessed from that wall's name: the Servian Wall. According to legend, this wall was built by King Servius Tullius around 900 years previously, when a man could comfortably ride across the Roman 'empire' in a day, and still have time for a good afternoon nap. Since then, the population of the city has grown from around 10,000 to around 1.5 million inhabitants. (It's hard to tell exactly – not everyone in Rome declares their presence to the authorities, and the authorities are not that interested in counting anyone apart from those eligible for conscription or the grain dole.)

Even the thousands of hectares enclosed by the Aurelian Walls do not protect the full sprawl of the city, but there can be no doubt that any barbarian invader getting this far will be suitably dumbfounded by the challenge of getting any further. The walls are brick-faced concrete that stand anywhere between 8 and 16 metres high with defensive towers every hundred paces – and even more formidable defences have been built alongside and over gates such as the Porta Appia. (Most gates in the Aurelian Walls are named after the roads that pass through them.) In fact, another of the contributions of the ill-fated Maxentius was to raise the size of the city walls to their present elevation. The original wall was built in just five years and was something of an ad hoc job – any buildings in the way of the wall were simply incorporated into the structure, so tidying things up in later years was probably a good idea.

The Porta Appia

Give a salute to the most impressive building project in all of third-century Europe as you pass through the walls by the Porta Appia, and imagine how much harder it would be to pass through if you were a hostile invader. The twin towers (over 20 metres tall) over the double-arched gate would be bristling with bowmen, javelineers and siege engines. Even if you did smash your way in, you would be trapped between two parallel walls stretching 20 metres into the city up to the so-called Arch of Drusus – with missiles raining down from above the whole time.

Whether a tourist or barbarian invader, you are not going to get a lot of time to admire the Arch of Drusus. Anyone standing still in

A Troubled Reign

Marcus Aurelius Valerius Maxentius (AD 283–312) was one of those emperors who lived in interesting times – he was perhaps the only emperor whose own father tried to depose him, and the most distinguished occupant of his family tomb is his son, who died young in suspicious circumstances. While Maxentius was the legitimate heir to the empire, he had limited support from the army, much of which supported the son of the successful general Constans. Eventually Maxentius met his fate at the hands of that son, the usurper Constantine (later Constantine the Great), at the Battle of the Milvian Bridge in AD 312. His troubled reign has left Rome with two legacies: a villa complex outside the city walls and a huge basilica that is the largest building in the Roman Forum.

the middle of the street is going to get short shrift either way, as this is one of the busiest streets outside of central Rome. Therefore, it is best to actually pass under one of the triple arches of this monument before stepping aside from the flow of humanity and looking back. At just over 7 metres high, the arch was probably quite impressive before it was dwarfed by the Porta Appia. While local tradition attributes the arch to Drusus, a son of the Emperor Tiberius, this is improbable.

Whomever the monument was constructed for seems to have come to a bad end as the arch is partly unfinished, and the authorities show it so little respect that these days a branch of the Aqua Marcia runs right over the top. A pity, for while much of the arch is of travertine stone (Rome's go-to building material), some of the columns are of Numidian marble. There is, by the way, a proper arch dedicated to Drusus, off to the north-west, near the Baths of Caracalla.

The Baths of Commodus

While we are on the topic of baths, it is time to wrap up this long walk with a soothing dip in hot water. A good bet might seem the Piscina Publica off to the left, just before the Porta Capena. Alas, this 'public swimming pool' now exists only as the place name for a nondescript residential and commercial district. The pool itself is long gone; indeed, the writer Festus stated that even in his day (the

Bad Emperor, Good Baths

Oddly enough, some of Rome's worst emperors have produced some really good baths. Nero's baths are famously luxurious, and Caracalla produced a truly spectacular set of baths that are destinations in themselves. Commodus was the disastrous son of the Emperor Marcus Aurelius who – among his other hare-brained acts – attempted to rename Rome as Colonia Commodiana. At the end of the year AD 192, Commodus was quietly strangled by an assassin hired by his nearest and dearest family members. Before this emperor's very timely demise, one of Commodus' lackeys had constructed the Baths of Commodus.

late second century AD), 'only the name exists – the thing itself is no more'. Fortunately, in Rome a good public bath is never far away.

Finish your walk at the Baths of Commodus, a refreshingly decadent bathing complex near the Porta Capena, ideally situated at the end of your long walk for a long soak to wash away the dust of the road.

THE TWENTY-FIRST CENTURY WALK

Some things never change. Sixteen hundred years later, the Alban Hills – now known to the locals as the Colli Albani – remain a cool, peaceful retreat from the noise and heat of Rome. The mansions of the wealthy and powerful still dot the hillsides. The most spectacular of these is the Castel Gandolfo on a hillock overlooking the Alban Lake. The owner of this magnificent residence is the Pope, who uses it as a summer refuge. The history of this site goes back well before the papacy, as the Emperor Domitian had the same idea of using this spot as a restful getaway. The ruins of his summer palace lie beneath Castel Gandolfo, and some archaeologists have speculated that the remains of the legendary Alba Longa lie beneath.

It would take considerable persuasion to launch a serious archaeological dig on this site, for the ground level contains some magnificent architecture, including buildings by Gian Lorenzo Bernini. Few know that the famous seventeenth-century sculptor was also an architect, although a visit to his exquisite Church of St Thomas will certainly persuade any doubters. Where Domitian's villa once stood are now the famed Barberini Gardens, which have the restrained elegance that only centuries of careful gardening can attain. Add graceful fountains and breathtaking views, and you can see why the popes wanted to keep the place to themselves until Pope Francis decided that this bounty should be shared with the public. Today, the gardens and much of the summer residence are also open to the public.

Another thing that has not changed is the area's reputation for fine wines. Since the 1970s, Alban wines have been within the Colli Albani DOC (*denominazione di origine controllata*). This means that the production of the wines is strictly controlled, and the wines must pass a quality and taste test before being unleashed upon the world. Wine tours are available for the dedicated oenophile, who will particularly appreciate the white wines made from the Malvasia grapes that are a local speciality.

Non-pedestrians might like to cheat by going away from Rome to visit Lake Nemi, which remains as beautiful as when it first attracted the decadent Caligula to its shores. Time has not been kind to the Temple of Diana, which is closed to the public (although a hired guide can take visitors through the ruins). Caligula's pleasure barges were raised from the lake in the 1930s and housed in a purpose-built museum. Regrettably, in 1944 some officer in the US Army decided that these ships constituted a threat to the free world. Although only lightly shelled by artillery, this seems to have been enough to set the museum afire, and these priceless ships were destroyed in the blaze. One of the mosaics from the ships ended up as a coffee table in New York before its provenance was discovered and the piece repatriated.

Those wanting to walk down the Appian Way to Rome should do so on a Sunday when only pedestrians are allowed. (At other times bicycles are a useful alternative.) The original paving stones testify to the durability of Roman craftsmanship and the remains of ancient tombs can still be seen at the roadside.

The most impressive of these remains the Tomb of Caecilia Metella, which we have already discussed. The excellent craftsmanship of the structure has seen it pass largely intact through the ages. No one knows what became of Caecilia, but she was probably no longer in residence even in the Middle Ages when the tomb became a mini castle used to extract tolls from travellers using the Appian Way. Today, the site is one of the most visited tourist sites outside central Rome – still, after all these millennia, fulfilling its original purpose of impressing visitors with the power and wealth of ancient Rome's Caecilian family.

The last ten miles of the Appian Way are now within a massive archaeological park that includes the Tomb of Caecilia, the Catacombs and the Villa of Maxentius. Even the aqueducts remain in view magnificently displayed in their own section: the *Parco degli Acquedotti*, where the peaceful scene is regularly disrupted by film crews using the location to shoot another sword-and-sandal epic against an authentically Roman background. The Nymphaeum of Egeria is also there and the water still flows from the spring (largely due to the heroic efforts of conservationists who prevented the area from being 'developed' to accommodate the expanding city of modern Rome.)

As before, it is also possible to wander through the Villa of Maxentius, but unlike the ancient tourist, modern visitors can also examine the huge formerly underground cistern that supplied the complex with water. Another stopping point is the Quo Vadis church where divine intervention is alleged to have ceased St Peter's flight from Nero's persecutors. The Porta Appia also still stands, now renamed the Porta San Sebastiano and looking even more formidable after some medieval enhancements to its battlements. There's a museum within the walls, but the mosaics there are modern reconstructions.

Still, don't stand in the middle of the road to admire the Arch of Drusus – this remains today one of the busiest roads in Rome and traffic is now faster and deadlier than the average ox-cart. Sadly, two of the three arches of the 'Drusus' memorial have gone, giving the remains a slightly forlorn appearance.

Like the Piscina Publica before them, the Baths of Commodus have vanished without trace, so today's visitor must resort to the facilities within one of the several hotels in the area or take the Metro san Giovanni to travel further into the modern city.

REGIO XIII: THE AVENTINE AND THE DOCKS

Working Rome

Today's walk begins on the Aventine Hill. For a long time, this hill was both inside and outside Rome. There's a long history behind this strange dichotomy and because it tells us a lot about the city that we will be exploring, it's worth looking at it more closely. The question is: 'What is the city of Rome and what is merely territory held by Rome?' To find the answer, look for the white stones called *cippi*. Where you see one of these, you'll probably be able to see one or two more dotted along an imaginary line. They mark the *pomerium* – the sacred boundary between 'Rome' and 'not Rome'. For most of its history, the Aventine has been outside the *pomerium*.

Note that you don't cross the *pomerium* – ever! Doing so means that you are technically invading Rome and will be treated as a sacrilegious marauder for the very brief remainder of your life. It's just as well, then, that the *pomerium* is not a continuous line enclosing the city or the inhabitants would starve to death. The gates represent gaps in the *pomerium* through which one can legitimately pass. However, except with vanishingly few exceptions, you can only legitimately pass if you are not carrying a weapon.

Weapons of any kind are forbidden within the *pomerium* – even a butcher is forbidden to step more than four paces from his stall while carrying a knife, since after that distance the knife ceases to

A TEMPLE OF THE BONA DEA

B TEMPLE OF DIANA ON THE AVENTINE

C EMPORIUM

D HOREA (Waterhouse)

E MONTE TESTACCHIO

F BATHS OF SURA

be a tool and becomes a weapon. The attendants of a magistrate known as lictors carry a bundle of rods (symbolizing the magistrate's power to punish) wrapped around an axe (the power to execute). Yet within the *pomerium*, lictors carry only the rods.

This is also a major reason why Julius Caesar was assassinated where and when he was. The senate usually meets within the *pomerium*, but on this occasion they were meeting at the Theatre of Pompey, which is outside it. Now, when you stab a dictator during a senate meeting, you are, by definition, using a weapon … and if you do that within the *pomerium*, the dictator's friends can legitimately add sacrilege to the host of other charges they'll be bringing against you.

What this has to do with the Aventine Hill is that for much of the history of Rome, the Aventine was *of* Rome but was not technically 'Rome'. And that's because the people of the Aventine very much wanted it that way. The Aventine is often called 'The People's Hill'. It does not have the grand architecture or civic spaces of places like the Palatine because by tradition the Aventine is where Rome's working classes lived and worked. In the imperial era this has changed somewhat, and although the popular perception remains, the fact is that there are several very substantial villas on the Aventine. Many of Rome's real working classes now live further downhill near the Emporium or have crossed the river for cheaper homes in the Transtiberim district.

The Remoria

This duality of Aventine versus Palatine is as old as Rome itself, so the best point to start today's walk is at the Saxa – an outcrop of rock on the hill looking north towards the racetrack of the Circus Maximus. There's a temple to the Good Goddess (the *Bona Dea*) located nearby, but the main reason for starting the walk here today is that this rocky outcrop is commonly held to be the site of the Remoria – a place sacred to Remus, the twin brother of Romulus. When the twins were preparing to found their new city, Romulus felt that the best site was the Palatine Hill. Remus vehemently disagreed and advocated the Aventine.

Both brothers started building energetically. Plutarch, in his *Life of Romulus*, says that Remus established the district on the Aventine, which in his day was called the Rignarium, while Romulus laid out a city on a small grid that was later called Roma Quadrata. It was clear that only one of these proto-settlements could be the city proper, so the pair proposed to let the gods decide which hill should become the centre of the new settlement. Remus took his place on the Aventine Hill on the Remoria, where the rocky outcrop gave a clear view of any heavenly manifestations. He saw six vultures – a clear sign of divine favour. When informed of this, Romulus retorted that he had seen twelve vultures. This was a blatant lie, so Remus went to confront his brother about it. While the pair were debating, the twelve vultures in question decided to show up – for real this time, thus handing Romulus the win.

The Secession of the Plebs

During the early history of the Republic in the fifth century BC, Rome was ruled by the patrician class and largely for the benefit of the patrician class. Finally, infuriated by the various abuses of their so-called betters, the plebeians of Rome more than once abandoned the city en masse in a very literal walkout. As we have seen, the Aventine was not technically part of Rome, so the plebs had left 'Rome' and its remaining population to their own devices. As the discomfited patricians now discovered, this meant that they had the temples and basilicas of Rome, but the plebs had the bakeries and laundries. There was also no question of taking the Aventine by force because even though the patricians had the officers, the plebs had the rest of the army. Negotiations followed. Thereafter, accompanied by some very hefty concessions, the people returned – but not before enshrining the idea of the Aventine as a practical counterbalance to the snobs on the Palatine.

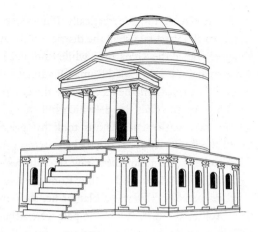

Remus was understandably bitter about the way things had transpired. His quarrel with Romulus developed into blows and then into a full-scale riot. In the course of this fracas both Remus and Faustulus, the foster-father of the twins, were killed. A remorseful Romulus interred the pair on Remus' Hill, the Aventine, at the Remoria (Plutarch, *Life of Romulus* 10).

The Temple of Diana on the Aventine

After paying respects to the memory of Remus, we proceed westwards. The road takes us to one of the oldest temples in Rome and the most important temple of the Aventine Hill, the *Aedes Dianae in Aventino* (the Temple of Diana on the Aventine). The building you will see here was extensively remodelled by the Emperor Augustus, but the foundations of the original were laid by Servius Tullius, the sixth king of Rome in about 550 BC.

> *Servius wanted to extend his city's power through diplomacy as well as by brute force, and at the same time add an ornament that would boost the prestige of Rome. At that time much was being made of the Temple of Artemis in Ephesus and how it*

had been built through the cooperation of all the states of Asia
[Minor]. Servius had cultivated guest-friendship with the heads
of the local Latin tribes and pointed out that they all worshipped
the same gods and worked well together. By hammering away
at this point he eventually got the Latin tribes to join with the
Romans in constructing a temple to Diana in Rome. Thus he got
the Latins to tacitly admit what they had so often disputed in
war – that Rome was now predominant.

Livy, *Ab Urbe Condida* (1.45)

The foundation day of this temple – traditionally 13 August – is still celebrated in many Italian towns (Statius, *Silvae* 3.60). The rites established here in the Temple of Diana were the template for ceremonies at other temples, not just in Rome but throughout Italy. Partly in recognition of this, Augustus installed in this temple a bronze column restating the ancient compact between Rome and the Latin peoples. There are also several statues of Diana in the temple – one is modelled on the one in the famed temple in Ephesus – and here can also be found what is alleged to be the oldest sundial in Rome.

If temples are your thing, the Aventine boasts a greater variety of temples than anywhere else in Rome. Within the *pomerium*, only

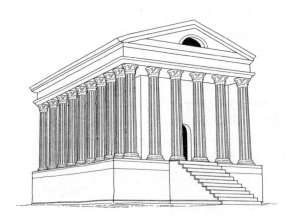

the temples of approved Roman gods are permitted. But because the Aventine was for so long outside the 'official' Rome, here one can find temples to Gallic, Egyptian, Phoenician and Scythian gods – the divine equivalent of Rome's multinational population.

The Servian Wall

Outside the Temple of Diana (a good Roman goddess), the road slopes downwards towards another reminder of the reign of King Servius Tullius. This reminder circles much of the ancient city: the Servian Wall, which was for centuries Rome's only defence against foreign invasion. As a reminder of how small Rome was when the walls were built, the Servian Wall (still Rome's penultimate line of defence) encloses just 500 acres, compared with the 2,500 acres of the more modern Aurelian Wall. The walls are of tufa, a mixture of volcanic ash and rock powder that has the handy property of hardening into solid rock upon exposure to the air. This means that tufa can be mined like loam but hardens like concrete once it has been above ground for a while.

As one gets to the further edge of the district of the Piscina Publica with its disappointing lack of public swimming pools, the road hits a small valley on the flank of the Aventine. The Servian Wall is built along the edge of this depression to take advantage of the natural extra height this gives the ramparts. To leave the Aventine, one must pass through the Porta Raudusculana, the Gate of the Bronze Horns. Why the gate is so called is explained by the writer Valerius Maximus:

> As the Praetor [a Roman magistrate second only to the consul] *Cippus was leaving through the gate as commander of an army, a prodigy of a new and unheard-of kind befell him. Suddenly horns sprouted from his head.*
>
> Valerius Maximus, *The Deeds and Sayings of Famous Men* (5.6.3)

The Sacred Boundary

The word *pomerium* comes from the early Italian words that later Latin would read as 'post-murum', that is 'beyond the walls'. In many cities of the region, even before Rome was founded, the *pomeria* had a practical purpose, this was the space beyond the walls that had to be kept clear of construction so that the city's defenders could have a clear field of fire. In Rome the *pomerium* has several other purposes, for it is a symbolic and religious boundary as well as a practical one. In fact, sometimes it is symbolic and religious even where there is no physical boundary.

Priests and seers were called into conference to explain what the gods were trying to tell the Romans by means of this startling development. Eventually it was decided that the horns were an omen signifying that when Cippus returned to the city, he would be crowned king of Rome. Since the Romans had only recently gotten rid of their kings and were determined to remain a republic, this was very bad news – not least to Cippus himself, who was as firm a republican as any of his fellow countrymen.

> *To prevent this from happening, he voluntarily and permanently went into exile. This gesture of worthy sacrifice bestowed upon him substantial glory, which is preferable to that earned by any of Rome's seven kings. As testimony to the grace of his sacrifice, bronze horns are affixed to the gate through which he had passed and the space thus enclosed is called the Raudusculana.*

Ibid.

The Docks

And so through the gate and to the Emporium after which all the emporia in the world are named. This was originally just an open space alongside a wharf abutting the River Tiber. It was where traders bringing goods upriver to Rome would unload their wares and merchants looking to get a jump on the competition would gather to meet them. In 193 BC this ad hoc arrangement was converted into a regular market, and since we are talking about the wholesale trade here, several substantial warehouses (*horrea*) were built behind the Emporium to house the goods thus purchased.

Originally the Emporium was a relatively modest affair to which merchants brought sacks of salt from the salt pans of Ostia, figs from North Africa and grain from Sicily. These days the Roman complex runs almost a Roman mile south from the Porta Trigemina in a maze of wharves, quays and warehouses – a rough area into which unwary tourists may wander and never emerge.

It's worth hooking up with a larger group – perhaps the retinue of a wealthy merchant – to see the docks, because much more than mundane items such as salt and corn are to be found in the complex. This part of the city is the receptacle into which the treasures of empire are poured for later redistribution around the city. For example, there's the rare and mysterious fabric, silk, imported from some distant and unknown location far away in the Orient and made of some unknown and unreproducible material. One thing is certain, the

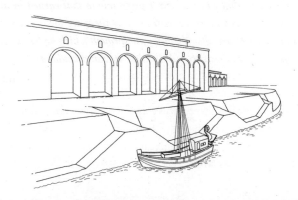

smoothly elegant cloth is superior to anything produced in Europe. Many an aristocratic Roman who affects the simple woollen toga of his forebears has under that a smooth silk *subcingulum* (a little thing tied beneath) – the Roman equivalent of luxury underpants.

Other luxury goods arriving here include Persian slippers, Parian marble and pepper from India, the latter being literally worth its weight in gold – if sold at a discount. Yet in some ways more impressive are the goods that the Romans receive in bulk, and none more so than *garum* sauce with which the Romans like to slather their meals. 'As the white surrounds the saffron-coloured yolk, let *garum* from the Spanish mackerel surround the egg' suggests the poet Martial in *Satires* (13.40). And not just egg – pork, game birds and even gruel are regularly flavoured by this powerful condiment.

As Martial points out, the *garum* shipped to the Emporium comes mainly from Spain these days, although the Levant and North Africa produced their fair share of the stuff back in the day. There's a regular convoy of ships bringing it upriver, each laden with amphorae full of the stuff. While Roman traders would love to produce *garum* locally, Rome lacks the key ingredients for its manufacture: long hours of constant sunlight and offshore shoals that produce an abundance of small fish.

To get some idea of the size of the *garum* trade, note that *garum* arrives in amphorae each containing around 72 litres of the condiment, and it's cheaper to make new amphorae at the source than to clean and re-export the empties. So these empties are taken to a spot just inland from the Emporium and dumped, along with other containers that once held olive oil and the little flasks holding opium imported from the East. Depositing containers on the top of this particular dump is quite an achievement, because over the centuries the mound has grown to a mini-mountain that is now well over 120 Roman feet – higher than Trajan's Column in the centre of Rome. Rather than ascend this man-made monster, consider taking a slow circumambulation of a thousand paces or so around the roughly triangular base. Pause behind the Galban warehouse to wonder at the line of workers adding yet more amphorae to the pile as the state

Making *Garum*

Which small fish are used for *garum* production is not important, although connoisseurs might maintain that they can tell if a particular batch was made with mackerel, anchovy or sardine. Tuna is also sometimes used, although tuna is a very substantial fish, so only the intestines are required. Once one has the necessary fish (or a basket-load of tuna guts), one needs to drop them into a shallow pool of briny water heated by direct sunlight and leave the lot there to ferment. Within a few days, the ingredients have combined into a glutinous mass that can be salted, strained and packed for export. At one time, the particularly finely strained form of *garum* was called *liquamen*, but these days the two terms are generally used interchangeably. The merchants lurking at the Emporium are particularly on the lookout for *garum* from Gades or New Carthage where the best *garum* is produced, although a sub-group of traders look for kosher *garum* to feed to Rome's large Jewish community.

reserve of olive oil is transferred to larger containers for redistribution.

There's a reason why the amphorae in this mound are mostly olive oil or *garum* containers, and that's because their fatty contents have saturated the baked clay. When no longer used for their original purpose, amphorae that have held wine or wheat are crushed into fine rubble and mixed into concrete to reinforce the cement. This doesn't work with *garum* or oil containers. Instead of getting *opus signinum* (a waterproof concrete used in pavements, baths and roofing), one gets a mixture of inferior concrete and soap produced by the interaction of fat from the clay and the lime, which is an essential ingredient of Roman cement.

If you are what you eat, the Romans are mostly Egyptian. That's because a lot of the wheat that arrives in Rome comes from Egypt. It comes to the Emporium in barges, for the huge seagoing grain tankers of the Egyptian trade would struggle to get this far up the Tiber. Every year over a quarter of a million tons of grain arrives in the city – an estimated eight months' worth of this arriving from Egypt (according to the historian Josephus who wrote in the first century AD). That's not the only Egyptian influence on the city either – several city squares and at least two racetracks sport Egyptian obelisks looted over the centuries.

The Pyramid of Cestius

Perhaps the most bizarre example of turning Egyptian, though, lies a bit further south-west on this walk. It's a large pyramid faced in white marble that, at 125 Roman feet, is only slightly shorter than the pile of crushed amphorae several hundred metres away. The detour to view this pyramid takes us right back to the Aurelian Walls – so exactly back in fact that the pyramid bisects the wall, sitting half within the city's defences and half outside. The base is over 100 feet long and the builders of the wall were not going to pass up the opportunity of making their task just that much shorter.

This isn't the only pyramid tomb in Rome – there's another outside the walls on the way to the Vatican Hill, but the one here is the more spectacular of the pair. It is possible to speculate that this particular pyramid isn't actually Egyptian at all. A keen historian

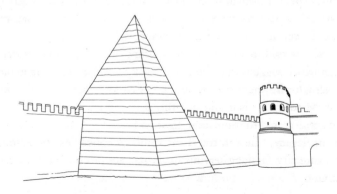

might note that at the time of the edifice's construction, Rome was probing south of Egypt to the African kingdom of Meroë, and the people of that nation built pyramids even more enthusiastically than the Egyptians – in fact, they have almost twice as many. Furthermore, Meronian pyramids have the same slender shape as the Pyramid of Cestius, rather than the more squat form of their much larger Egyptian counterparts. Was the tomb's creator inspired by these?

The occupant of the pyramid is one Gaius Cestius Epulo. We know a lot about him, because the purpose of the tomb was to ensure that he will never be forgotten. (This has worked so far.)

According to the inscriptions on the side, Gaius was the son of Lucius Cestius. He served as a tribune of the plebs and later reached the rank of praetor. (Since praetors sometimes had military commands, Gaius Cestius might even have been to Meroë himself on one of those Roman expeditions to the south.) He was a member of the voting tribe of Publilia (a rural constituency) and a proud officer in the Epulones religious corporation.

There are four traditional religious colleges in Rome. For prestige, one should aim for the colleges of the Pontiffs or Augurs. Those of a clerkly disposition might prefer the college charged with looking after the sacred texts of Rome. But no college has the perks of the Epulones, which is charged with overseeing the sumptuous banquets that are a major part of Roman religious festivals. Given how fiercely contractors compete to supply food and facilities for these banquets, it's a pretty poor corporation member who cannot eat free and well from kickbacks from the grateful winners.

We are told that construction of the pyramid took just under a year, which suggests that Gaius had stockpiled some of the materials needed for his memorial before he passed away. Construction was supervised by his heir and one of his freedmen. It is not unusual for the deceased to stipulate in their will that the heir can only take up his legacy if he constructs the tomb of his benefactor. Also, it is customary for long-serving slaves to be freed on their master's demise.

The Ostian Gate

To re-enter the Aurelian Walls, follow them along for a couple of hundred paces to the Ostian Gate. This is a typical gateway of travertine stone, a double archway topped with formidable towers. This gate is, as ever, named for the road that enters the city through it – in this case the road from Ostia, fourteen Roman miles down the river, which the road mostly runs alongside. We are not going to go as far as the Servian Wall and the Porta Trigemina, but we'll instead stop to look at the Atrium of Cacus.

> *He [Cacus] dwelled in a vast cavern with deep recesses,*
> *So hidden the wild creatures could barely find it.*
> *Over the entrance hung human arms and skulls,*
> *And the ground bristled with whitened bones.*

> Ovid, *Fasti* (1.554)

The monstrous Cacus came unstuck when he tried to rob cattle from Hercules who was passing through with a herd that he himself had robbed in one of his famous Labours. When he realized that Hercules had discovered the theft, Cacus blocked his cave with a

Trajan and Sura

The Baths of Sura date back to the time of the Emperor Trajan (AD 98–117) and were either built by his friend Lucius Licinius Sura or constructed by Trajan himself and dedicated to his friend's memory. Like Trajan, Sura came from Spain and he served three times as consul in Rome. When there were rumours that Sura was plotting to kill Trajan, the emperor responded by visiting Sura without his bodyguards, dining at his house and then getting a shave on the premises – the latter less for tonsorial purposes than to demonstrate that Trajan trusted Sura even with a razor held to his throat. These baths are another sign of the close relationship between Sura and his emperor.

stone so large that 'a ten-yoke of oxen could not have budged it'. The enraged Hercules tossed the stone aside like a pebble and the might of Cacus proved far less mighty than the olive-wood club with which Hercules pounded him into the ground – much to the delight of the locals whom Cacus had victimized for so long.

After contemplating the scene of that one-sided struggle, loop back towards the Aventine and finish the day with a soak in the Baths of Sura.

It's possible to get a shave and also a massage at Sura's baths, and while there you can ease any aching muscles in the *cella tepidaria* – a lower-level warm room that has recently been renovated and restored.

THE TWENTY-FIRST CENTURY WALK

The Temple of Diana on the Aventine is now gone, so this is not to be confused with another location of the same name in north Rome situated within a pleasantly green area just outside the Porta Pinciana, another of the gates within the Aurelian Walls that is still in use today.

However, those wanting to start a walk on the Aventine are spoiled for choice as to how to get there. Firstly, there's a large railway station nearby, the Termini Porta San Paolo, a bus stop of the same name, and a nearby Metro station, Pyramide. Since the Porta San Paolo is the Ostia Gate renamed and Pyramide refers to the Pyramid of Cestius, it's not hard to work out that you're in the right area. In fact, you can still now walk along the Via Ostia in its new incarnation as the Via Ostiense and through the Porta San Paolo/Ostia Gate (assuming you survive the traffic).

Regrettably, there are now no known *cippi* to mark the *pomerium* to prevent inadvertent sacrilege on your part, but rest assured that the penalties for so doing have become considerably less draconian over the centuries. The Pyramid of Cestius remains in place intact and as impressive as ever, and its occupant would have been delighted to know that the road alongside it now also bears his name, the Via Caio Cestio. Several other famous figures have joined Cestius in the neighbourhood, with the grave of British poet Percy Bysshe Shelley being of particular interest to English-speaking visitors. However, only the tomb of Cestius is a small museum where – unlike fourth-century visitors – tourists can now also explore the interior. (Sadly, the other pyramid tomb in Rome has now gone – another victim of the regrettable tendency of medieval popes to treat their cultural inheritance as a stone quarry for pet building projects.)

At the end of the Via Caio Cestio is the unmistakable bulk of the Monte Testaccio, still massive, although now a lot grassier and surrounded by smart cafés and boutiques. These days, a place of greenery and pleasant walkways, the man-made mound has also served as an artillery platform in the Napoleonic wars and as a stand-in for the mound of Golgotha in Easter celebrations. In keeping with the theme of tombs just outside the old Aurelian Walls, there's now a substantial cemetery just to the south.

These days, goods coming into twenty-first century Rome use the railroad, so where there were once miles of docks and warehouses along the Tiber, there is now a grassy track with a rural feel to it. This finally leads to blocks of apartment houses and a graffiti-covered sign announcing the site of the old Emporium, with the modern version of the Sublician Bridge (the original was built over 2,000 years previously) just in sight upriver from there. Crossing this bridge leads to another riverside track popular with cyclists and joggers.

Overall, the modern pedestrian tourist may do better to skip the walk to the Tiber and instead head southwards for a glimpse of ancient, ancient Rome unavailable to the fourth-century tourist. This is La Scatola Archeologica (the Archaeological box) found within an apartment complex. People have been living here for a long time. Some structures date to the eighth century BC, there are the remains of a fortified tower (sixth century) and another six layers of habitation dating through the imperial era, making this small museum the most compressed bit of history in the whole of Rome. After this visit, loop back to the Porta San Paolo (Ostia Gate) and from there follow the Viale di Porta Ardeatina as it runs alongside a standing stretch of the Aurelian Walls right back to the Aventine.

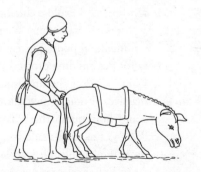

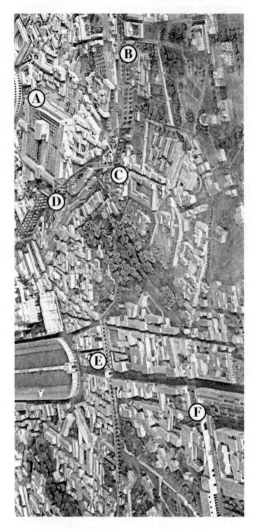

A TEMPLE OF CLAUDIUS

B MACELLUM MAGNUM

C CASTRA PEREGRINA

D NERONIAN AQUEDUCT SPUR

E PORTA CAPENA

F BATHS OF CARACALLA

REGIO II: THE CAELIAN HILL

Millionaires' Row

The settlement of the Caelian Hill is recounted by the Roman historian Livy. The population originally lived in Alba Longa until that city was captured by Servius Tullius, the sixth king of Rome.

> King Servius went on to say, 'My course of action will bring good fortune and happiness to the Roman people and myself, and also to you, people of Alba. I intend to transfer the entire population of Alba Longa to Rome. The rights of citizenship I shall bestow to the plebeians, and enrol the nobles in the senate. We shall be made one city, and one nation.'

> Grabbing whatever they could carry, the Albans left their city, their hearths, their household gods and the homes in which they had been born and raised … The emigrants filled the streets, and as neighbour recognized neighbour their shared misery led to fresh outbursts of tears.

> Alba's fall of Alba helped the rise of Rome. The citizen population doubled, the Caelian Hill was brought within the city bounds, and to encourage settlement there King Tullius chose it for the site of his palace, and lived at that location thereafter.

> Livy, *Ab Urbe Condita* (29-30 passim)

To be honest, the Caelian Hill is really more of a ridge, and not a very high one at that. It is just over two Roman miles long and less than a sixth of that in width. For most of what might laughingly be called its 'height', it is about the altitude of the man-made spoil heap of the amphora pile beside the docks. At its peak it soars all of 157 feet over the valley of the Circus Maximus and the Flavian Amphitheatre (aka the Colosseum). Until it received its present name (the etymology of which is much disputed), the hill was known as 'oak hill' since oak trees made up much of the abundant greenery that the hill's well-heeled inhabitants have been careful to preserve.

One suggestion is that the Caelian gets its present name from *caelum* (heaven) – and for some of the inhabitants, this is certainly as close as one can get in Rome. Downhill at the base of the Esquiline, the working classes are packed densely into the large apartment buildings known as *insulae* with around four people to a room. (Many Romans go from birth to death without ever being in a room – or anywhere else – on their own. It's why there is no Latin word for 'murder' – an act that requires a degree of privacy. Latin does have *homicidium* – homicide – but there were usually witnesses to that.) The entire Caelian Hill is home to about as many Romans as those who live on a single short street of *insulae* and on the Caelian there are around two fountains for every four households – with most of these fountains redundant as the houses have their own water piped in.

Pliny the Elder, writing in the first century AD, spends a portion of book 36.7 of his *Natural History* venting on the profligacy of the houses of the wealthy, with special scorn for those on the Caelian.

> He [a Roman knight called Mamurra] *was the first to cover his house on the Caelian Hill entirely in walls veneered with marble. It's enough that this idea was invented by this scoundrel to make it totally improper. This is the Mamurra who was reviled by* [the poet] *Catullus, the Mamurra whose house proclaims even more loudly than Catullus could have done himself that 'he had taken all that Gaul had once owned.'*

[Mamurra was an officer under Julius Caesar – 'under' in all senses of the word if we are to believe the vituperative Catullus – who used his position to become obscenely rich through corrupt practices in the conquered province.] *'And by the way … he had columns in his house of solid Carystus and Luna marble.'* [Both being rare and mind-bogglingly pricey types of stone.]

Elsewhere Pliny adds indignantly: 'The laws were silent when these huge blocks of marble were dragged past the earthenware pediments of temples to a private house.'

A (Wealthy) Roman's Home

If you want to wander the shady streets of the Caelian to see how the other half live (actually, the top 1 per cent), this walk might prove something of a disappointment. In some parts of town, a *domus* will have a small business or two facing streetside – a tradesman's shop, for example. On the Caelian, the typical Roman *domus* presents a blank wall with the only break being a well-fortified door that opens outwards into the street. Rome does not have a police force and there's much to loot in a wealthy house. So, the doors open outwards because that makes bashing them in that much harder.

In his novel written in the second century AD, the writer Apuleius describes an incident that sums up the fears of those living behind these walls.

> *I was returning home from dinner … when in front of my host's house (I'm staying with Milo, your good fellow-citizen), I found some vicious thieves trying to force their way in, intending to smash the hinges and break the door apart. All the carefully fastened bolts had been violently torn away and the men were planning among themselves how to murder the people inside.*

> Apuleius, *The Golden Ass* (3.5)

Fear of such incidents not only means that the residences of the wealthy are well defended, but also that anyone strolling down the street paying close attention to the houses on each side will probably find himself confronted by several large and unsympathetic gentlemen who are eager to demonstrate why this is not a good idea. On the other hand, those with the connections to secure an invitation into one of these homes will discover that wealthy Romans have remarkably conformist ideas about domestic arrangements that go beyond perimeter defence.

The house – which is also generally the occupant's business premises – is also a religious centre for the *familia* that lives there. (*Familia* is wider than family, extending to include the servants, slaves, permanent guests and the pet dog.) This multiplicity of roles means that the house has public and private areas with entrance to both parts through a short, narrow entryway guarded by a beady-eyed doorman. This corridor opens into the atrium – a room generally open to the sky in the centre, with the roof arranged so that water drains inwards, often to a central pool (*impluvium*) that is sometimes a fishpond with fruit trees arranged around. (It says something of the Roman mentality that even the homes of the very wealthy also supply the occupants with food and water.)

Since the atrium is where visitors to the house will spend most of their time, this is where the most ostentatious displays of wealth and power are likely to be found, be they marble pillars or the funeral masks of ancestors stretching back through the generations. The peristyle (a sort of colonnaded verandah) towards the rear is sometimes a simpler affair depending on the taste of the occupant and his family, for apart from domestic servants, few members outside the family will get further than the room between the public and private sphere. This is the *triclinium*, which we could call a dining room, but if so, we might as well call the *Titanic* a tugboat.

The *triclinium* is elaborately decorated from the carved ceiling joists and panels to the murals and the intricate mosaics on the floor. It's where the *paterfamilias* entertains his guests; dinner topics might range from social networking to philosophy, business or political backstabbing. It's where the host makes the maximum effort to impress his guests with his wealth and power. By contrast, even the wealthiest have relatively spartan bedrooms. In the Roman view, a bedroom is for sleeping and sex. Almost every other function, from bowel movements to bathing to dining, is done in company. 'Alone time' is an alien concept.

Behind the bedrooms at the back may be a small garden (useful for growing herbs) and a kitchen. The kitchen is also a somewhat pokey affair, because in houses such as these, cookery is done by subordinates. These are generally slaves, so the facilities in the kitchen seldom match the magnificence of the meals prepared there. Fortunate slaves will have rooms above ground here. Others will sleep crammed into smaller basement accommodation – not everyone on the Caelian lives like a king.

The Temple of the Divine Claudius

Those without any other good excuse for being on the Caelian should head purposefully towards the Temple of the Divine Claudius, the point at the base of the hill from which we begin today's walk. Like most Roman emperors, the Emperor Claudius (AD 41–54) was made a god upon his demise. In the case of Claudius, this happened after eating poisonous mushrooms. Agrippina, the widow of Claudius, was suspected of having poisoned those mushrooms to secure the succession of her son, the unlovely Nero. It seemed a good idea for Agrippina to counter the scurrilous rumours that she had killed her husband by proving her wifely devotion with a splendid temple in her late husband's memory.

Since it was the declaration of her intentions that was important, Agrippina was in no hurry to finish the building and it was still incomplete when Nero, who had a famously tin ear for public opinion, decided instead to make the temple a decorative nymphaeum. This was to serve as an outlying building, part of the complex making up the splendid 'Golden House', which he was constructing for himself in the centre of Rome. (Agrippina was no longer around to object, as Nero had arranged her murder.)

A branch of the Aqua Claudia aqueduct was constructed to feed the fountains of the former temple and this is almost the only part of Nero's reconstructions to have survived. Nero's eventual successor, the Emperor Vespasian, demolished and repurposed most parts of Nero's Golden House and restored the temple to its proper function. However, the wealthy denizens of the Caelian appreciated the extra water for their fountains and fishponds, so the Arcus Neroniani branch of the Aqua Claudia remains, running just behind the temple.

From the Temple of Claudius, you have an excellent view of the colossal statue that gives the area of the Colosseum its name. However, this is a sight for another day, so turn instead to study the Porticus Claudia, a shaded walkway leading to the front of the Temple of the Divine Claudius. A connoisseur of temple design might be able to appreciate the elegantly prostyle hexastyle layout (architect-speak for six columns leading to the front), but for the average visitor this is simply a pleasant place to relax and appreciate the splendid flower beds in the gardens alongside.

There's a degree of bustle on the road running south alongside the temple. Just down this road is the Castra Peregrina. Also known as the Antonine Camp, this barracks is designed to accommodate soldiers who arrive in Rome on detachment from their duties elsewhere. (The centurion who accompanied St Paul to Rome probably stayed here on his arrival.)

Guardians of the Grain

The Castra Peregrina is also the base of the *Frumentarii*, those members of the military charged with securing the city's grain supply and its orderly distribution. In fact, these soldiers act as a sort of reserve force to assist the urban cohorts on occasions such as when there's a particularly restive crowd – for example, after the chariot races at the Circus Maximus. Because their duties take them all over the empire, the *Frumentarii* also act as couriers for the imperial bureaucracy and carry things like census reports along with estimates of how much wheat a particular province might be able to deliver in a given year.

The Macellum Magnum

As you pass under the arches of the Neronian extension of the Claudian aqueduct, you'll note that this is plumbed directly into the Antonine barracks. The emperors know that their power is ultimately based on the army and take good care of their soldiers. A few metres away, just on the other side of the aqueduct, lies one of Rome's greatest gourmet markets, the Macellum Magnum. This is one of Nero's better creations, albeit constructed with the cynical intent of garnering goodwill from the wealthy aristocrats on the hill.

Most markets in Rome are *nundinae* that, as the name says, appear as pop-up street markets every nine days. Very often these are direct-to-customer affairs in which local farmers take a day off to sell their produce in Rome. However, while the average *materfamilias* might be prepared to plan her family meals on a nine-day schedule, there is always a demand for those items that are needed unexpectedly or for when nothing but absolutely fresh will suit the diner's refined taste. For such situations, there is the *macellum*.

Unlike the mildly chaotic street markets of the *nundinae*, a *macellum* is a highly organized affair. For a start, if it's raining on

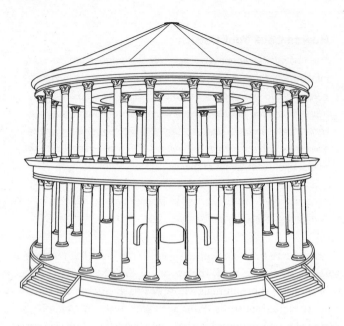

a street market one gets wet (and the vegetables there stay slightly fresher than they would otherwise). The *macellum* is an enclosed building, so shoppers stay dry. Indeed, in the case of the Macellum Magnum, this building is two storeys high with elegant arches and carved stonework. In most cases a *macellum* has a central circular area (the *tholos*) within a square structure. The Macellum Magnum is exceptional in that its two stories are completely circular in shape so that shoppers can literally wander around beneath the domed roof.

Within there is a series of small courts, eight in all, with two dedicated to meat and fish respectively. These areas require special attention because the meat needs to be kept clean and insect free, and there are special plumbing facilities for washing it. Much of this meat will be well out of the price range of the average Roman doing his grocery shopping. There might, for example, be thrushes (*turdes*) imported from Spain, since nothing says 'refined palate' more than a roasted songbird. Sows' udders are also much sought after, as well as those giant tasty snails from Africa.

How to Cook Your Ostrich

For boiling the sauce you need stock made from: pepper, mint, roasted cumin, celery seeds, raisin wine, honey, vinegar, garum, and a dash of oil. Put these in the pot and bring to the boil. Thicken the mix with wheat starch [amylum], *pour over the ostrich steaks cut to size and sprinkle with pepper. If you are going to sauté the ostrich in the sauce, add* Alica. [Not a female of that name, but a type of garlic.]

Apicius, *Cookbook* (Recipe 212)

If there has been an imperial spectacular at the arena in the Colosseum down the road, then some of the empire's latest victims may be on sale – those animals whose deaths so entertained the crowd end up as exotic foodstuffs. From elephant steaks to crocodile fillets or lumps of hippopotamus fat, the Romans don't let a lot go to waste.

Fish are best served fresh, so apart from lampreys pulled from the Tiber that morning, you might also find mullet, turbot and sea bass. There will be fewer of these than one might expect, because the wealthy own fishponds and their cooks trade fish among themselves. But look for oysters and mussels still living in seawater-filled basins cut into the marble counters, cuttlefish, sea urchins and octopus also. *Locusta*, by the way, are not locusts but a type of long-tailed lobster that is usually served in a delicious sauce.

Hardened gourmets might prefer to end the walk here and spend the rest of the day browsing the culinary delights on offer at the *macellum*. Especially as we have not yet even stepped outside to look at the even greater diversity of goods on offer in the stalls that cluster thickly around the main market itself. Otherwise, to continue the walk, detour slightly around the side of the market to contemplate the Arch of Dolabella – a reconstructed gate in the Servian Wall that Nero, with his usual delicacy in treating other people's memorials, co-opted as a part of his aqueduct extension.

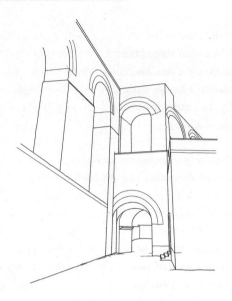

It is unknown whether this Dolabella was the son or merely a close relative of that Dolabella who married Cicero's daughter, but it is only the fame of the constructor that gives much significance to an otherwise mediocre piece of city furniture. Therefore, after briefly studying this and the Servian Wall, proceed towards the Caput Africae (a college for the training of imperial pages) and look around for a small park.

This was probably the location where ended one of Rome's most unlikely rebellions – that of workers at the imperial mint. There was once a mint at the base of the Caelian Hill, secondary to the main mint on the Capitoline Hill. This was probably because in Republican times any wealthy Roman had the right to convert his personal holdings into gold or silver coinage of his own design (but of a standard weight). The base of the Caelian was a handy location where a denizen of the Caelian could stroll down and see how his vanity coinage was coming along, as one does on an idle morning.

At the start of the reign of the Emperor Marcus Aurelius (AD 161–80), the quality of Roman coinage took a nosedive in quality. Since there seemed no other obvious reason for this, Aurelius challenged the head of the mint – the inappropriately named Felicissimus – to account for the gold that should have gone into the coins. Instead, Felicissimus brought out his fellow workers in a strike that rapidly degenerated into a savage little civil war. How that turned out was described by the emperor himself (who as it happens was born in a *domus* on the Caelian):

> *It seems as though Fate has ordained that all the wars that I wage and all other disruptions only get more challenging. I have just fought a most bitter struggle with rebels within the city. Under the leadership of Felicissimus, the most miserable of all my slaves, whom I had put in charge of the mint, the workers demonstrated a rebellious spirit. They have indeed been crushed, but with the loss of seven thousand men, some from the city camps, others treasury guards and boatmen.*

Victor, De Caesaribus: Marcus Aurelius (38)

The Baths of Caracalla

From the scene of this grim little battle, proceed down the Vicus Sulpicius and the Via Nova to the main attraction of the day: the Baths of Caracalla. Caracalla (AD 193–211) was born Lucius Septimius Bassianus and called himself Marcus Aurelius Antoninus. To avoid nomenclatural confusion, future generations have opted to call this emperor Caracalla after his habit of wearing the colourful Gallic cloaks of that name. Caracalla came to a messy end when one of his retinues chose to stab him at a vulnerable moment while he was on the road to Edessa (he had stopped for a bathroom break). The emperor's two lasting legacies were to make all free persons in the empire into Roman citizens and construct a massive set of baths near the Appian Way on the south side of the Caelian Hill in Rome. (The location was chosen in part to take advantage of the water from the recently constructed Marcian Aqueduct that enters Rome at this point.)

Anyone going to these baths just to wash is missing a great deal of what the baths have to offer. This is not just a place of running waters, but a huge leisure complex some 25 hectares in area. It accommodates more than 1,500 visitors at a time and somewhere just short of 10,000 people every day. Just the open-air bath alone is the size of an Olympic swimming pool.

The baths themselves were originally planned by Caracalla's father Septimius Severus. He died before construction was fully under way, and the project was then hijacked by his son who knew a superb public relations opportunity when he saw one. A luxury villa – belonging to one Pollio – was demolished to make room for the new complex. Thousands of prisoners captured in the British campaigns of Septimius Severus worked on the site, along with some 6,000 artisans. An estimated 6,300 cubic metres of marble went into the construction.

Several decorations from Pollio's villa were retained to adorn the new baths, including a group statue by the famed Apollonius of Tralles representing the death of Dirce. (A mythical queen of Thebes killed when her vindictive enemies tied her to the horns of a wild bull.)

This is not a trivial statue, being carved from a single lump of white marble 9 square metres at the base and standing just under 4 metres high. Yet this is just one of the many decorations dotting the grounds and gardens of the baths, for not only Caracalla but also his immediate successors competed to make the baths ever more ornate and impressive. The walls are mainly of brick (literally millions of them), but faced with marble and Egyptian granite and decorated with elaborate bas-reliefs and painted murals.

Most of the floor space is covered with intricate mosaics – look especially for the so-called 'Athletes' mosaic' from the *palestra* (exercise area). Here we find several dozen panels with depictions of over-muscled bronzed males. Some of these are aspirational images suggesting what a 98-pound weakling might become after repeated visits to the baths, but others are depictions of real athletes – mostly wrestlers – who have their names in the mosaic beside them.

Technically a *palestra* is an indoor arena for wrestling, but the *palestra* also has spaces for those who want to push weights, play a round of handball or simply lie, lathered in oil, while they get a

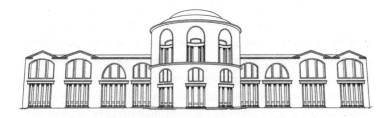

massage. The baths also have extensive gardens, carefully maintained by some of the host of slaves who maintain the complex, doing everything from building repairs to feeding around ten tons of firewood daily into the insatiable hypocausts that keep the bath water warm to fertilizing the flowers and looking after the clothes of the bathers.

The bathers might start with a dip in one of two lukewarm pools (there are also individual bathtubs, some in grey Egyptian marble) and then progress to the steam room with over half a dozen hot baths or steam rooms to choose from, with temperatures ranging from mildly warm to parboiled human. To stop cooking, one is advised to follow the chain of artificial waterfalls to the next room, the cold room, where one can plunge into water frigid enough to restore bodily temperature equilibrium. After that, one might like to get dried off and retire to one of the libraries on the grounds (choose the Greek or Latin library) for a quiet read before facing the evening. Alternatively, there are stands selling drinks and snacks, a barbershop, a museum and an odeon for musical performances. There is also a *parfumerie* for female visitors.

The baths are not merely the physical manifestation of the Latin proverb *mens sana in corpore sano* (a healthy mind in a healthy body), they are also an important part of a Roman's social routine. Meeting at a house immediately establishes a guest-host power dynamic of which the status-conscious Romans are immediately aware. Meeting at the baths puts everyone on an equal footing, although there is always the risk of social climbers who scuttle after lost balls during a game, praise the thrower's expertise and generally do all they can to secure a dinner invitation for the evening.

There are separate bath times for men and women, but as with many governmental edicts, Romans regard these as advisory. However, those contemplating bathing along with the opposite sex should be aware that the authorities frown upon this. Every second emperor passes an edict banning the practice of mixed bathing as deeply immoral, but just the fact that this ban has to be so constantly reissued tells us what the Romans think of the idea.

> *Wine, Venus and the baths corrupt our bodies*
> *But drinking, the baths and sex are what life is about.*

> Epitaph of Claudius Secundus of Ephesus, Rome, first
> century AD, *Corpus Inscriptionum Latinarum* (VI 15258)

THE TWENTY-FIRST CENTURY WALK

Many of the elegant mansions of the wealthy are still around on the Caelian, although not in recognizable form. Most have been largely dismantled and the masonry used for the profusion of churches on the hill. For example, the Basilica dei Santi Quattro Coronati is itself ancient (fifth century AD), but it is largely made from an even older villa that used to stand on the site. Much of the temple of Claudius has become the bell tower of St Peter and Paul, a church that stands on the site, while other relics from the temple can be viewed by those prepared to travel to the Glyptothek in Munich where they now reside. Of the temple itself, only the extensive base platform remains.

Other ancient stonework has gone into the Villa Celimontana, a large complex of buildings and parkland put in place when the hill was extensively re-landscaped during the sixteenth century. (There is now a summer jazz festival at the villa that hosts dozens of performances between June and September.)

It is, however, probable that one can access more aristocratic Roman houses now than was possible in the fourth century. If one starts on the Clivo di Scauro near the Colosseum, it is possible to view the surviving villas in the Case Romane del Celio tour (the Roman houses of the Caelian). Much of what can be visited today is underground due to the medieval habit of leaving rubbish outside, causing street levels to rise, but on the bright side, being underground has shielded these buildings from damage and decay.

Not much remains of the Castra Peregrina, but a modern visitor may have better luck with the Macellum Magnum. Although it has suffered destruction and rebuilding over the centuries, the present structure is at least evocative of what was once there. It is still a large circular building, but these days it is a church and sells salvation rather than sardines. The present form owes much to Theodore I (AD 642–9), but the foundations and much of the outer colonnade appear to be from the original market. It is still an impressively substantial building and looking at the circular colonnades and the alcoves within the arches, it is not hard to imagine the bustling market of yesteryear.

As a visitor might have done 1,600 years ago, this is a good moment to step around the corner to see if the Arch of Dolabella has become any more impressive over the centuries. It hasn't, but the remnants of the Aqua Marcia looming over the arch are quite spectacular, and it is always remarkable to gaze on something that Nero and Trajan probably also saw all those years ago.

Pause at the park at the top of the hill from where the excellent view of the Colosseum was enjoyed as much in antiquity as it can still be today. Then take your life in your hands by battling through the tangle of highways to the Terme di Caracalla, with the Antonine road alongside, as it was in antiquity. (There's an alternative walk that skips the Caelian altogether and instead goes along the urban section of the Appian Way from the forum to the baths, with a selection of ancient Roman sites along the way.)

The gardens remain and are as pleasant as ever, although at times very crowded. The baths still draw in thousands of visitors, although none of the pools have functioned since Rome went to the dogs during the sixth century AD. In AD 847 the baths were further damaged by an earthquake, which also further dilapidated the Colosseum. Thereafter, the medieval popes began to take an interest in the many objets d'art remaining at the baths, so many of these

– including the mosaic of the Athletes – can now be found across town in the Vatican. The famed sculpture of the death of Dirce has survived intact through the ages, but these days it is to be found in the National Archaeological Museum in Naples under the name of Farnese Bull. (It was a gift to the then king of Naples.)

Despite the predations of time and the papacy, the baths remain a highly impressive sight, deeply evocative of ancient Rome at the peak of its power. For almost a century now, these ruins have been used as the backdrop for artistic performances from opera to ballet to concerts of classical music. These performances happen under the stars almost every night in summertime, making it a wonderful way to finish the day's walk – for those who have the foresight to purchase tickets and bug spray beforehand.

REGIO III:
FROM THE COLOSSEUM TO
TRAJAN'S BATHS

Gladiators and Hot Water

We now move down from the Caelian, which is a very gentle descent given this hill's lack of height, and come to the valley between the Oppian and Caelian hills. In the earliest times, this, together with the Campus Martius, was part of the natural flood-plain for the Tiber's spring overflow. Today, preventing the river from reclaiming its ancient territory is a constant preoccupation of the aediles, city officials charged with maintaining Rome's infrastructure.

The ancient marsh at the foot of the Caelian has now been drained for centuries, but except for a period of dense inhabitation in the era of the late Republic, the area has never really been residential. The Romans like to live on their hills (partly due to the aforesaid floods) and the space between the hills is used for civic purposes. Today, the only indication of the valley bottom's former sogginess is a large fountain and a small stream that runs through well-fortified banks.

The Colosseum 'Temple' of Isis and Serapis

Today's walk starts on the Via Labicana at the archway leading to the sanctuary – not temple – after which Regio III is officially named (the full name of this area is Regio III Isis et Serapis).

A TEMPLE OF ISIS AND
   SERAPIS
B TEMPLE OF VENUS AND
   ROMA
C ARCH OF CONSTANTINE
D THE COLOSSUS

E THE FLAVIAN
   AMPHITHEATRE
   (THE COLOSSEUM)
F THE PORTICO OF LIVIA
G TRAJAN'S BATHS

Isis and Serapis, majestic and sublime though they may be, are not Roman gods but Egyptian imports. Indeed, the Romans are so ambivalent about Isis that in Republican times the shrine to the goddess on the Capitoline Hill was demolished in 53 BC by the city authorities. That fit of iconoclasm aside, the Romans treat Isis with a degree of caution, for worship of the goddess had been celebrated for around 2,000 years before the founding of Rome itself.

Just as Juno in the Roman pantheon is both the wife and sister of Jupiter, the king of the gods, so was Isis the wife and sister of the god Osiris. Osiris was killed by his evil brother Set and his body dismembered. Isis gathered up the parts, reassembled them and breathed life into the corpse long enough to copulate with it and beget a son called Horus. (Ancient mythology of whatever religion is not for the squeamish.) As a result of this tangled tale (the version given above has been brutally simplified), Isis is a mother deity with a foot in the worlds of both the living and the dead.

Because in Egypt the Caesars are regarded as the equivalent of the pharaohs, any current emperor is conflated with the god Horus

Templum vs 'Shrine'

In Rome, templum has a very strict meaning. It is a sacred space marked out by a priest called an augur, specifically for the purpose of divining the will of the gods through signs in the sky or the ground nearby. Obviously the augur would prefer to do this in a sacred place, but for the purposes of divination any hilltop can become a temporary templum. On the other hand, some places that are sacred in Rome cannot be used for augury and these, therefore, do not count as a templum. For example, there is no Temple of Vesta for the simple reason that augurs are male and men are not allowed into a shrine maintained solely by Vestal Virgins. Likewise, although a substantial structure, the sanctuary of Isis and Serapis cannot be used to divine the will of the city's gods and is therefore not a templum.

and his predecessors with Osiris. As mother, wife and sister to these deities, Isis is almost family, so the emperors these days treat her shrines with respect.

Serapis is a more interesting character, because he is almost but not quite Ra, the Egyptian sun god. (That's where the 'ra' bit in the middle of his name comes from.) At one time this deity went by the name of Osorapis and was a relatively obscure member of the Egyptian pantheon. Then Egypt came under the rule of the Hellenistic Ptolemies. By way of spreading Egyptian influence, the Ptolemies adopted Osorapis as Serapis, adapted him into a form more suited to Graeco-Roman worship and sent him and Isis out into the Mediterranean world as cultural ambassadors of the new Egypt.

Ptolemaic Egypt is no more, but the two gods still have a substantial number of worshippers. The shrine in Regio III is worth a visit for a look at the obelisks and Egyptian-themed statuary within. Those who believe in hedging their bets might like to offer a small sacrifice to Isis while there. This does not have to be anything elaborate – food such as fruit is quite acceptable, but don't offer onions (which, for reasons we need not go into here, devotees of Isis do not eat).

The Temple of Venus and Roma

From here, it may be a good idea to re-establish your credentials as a respectable follower of the gods of Rome. How better to do this than to pop across the way and visit the Temple of Roma, the divine personification of the city itself? Roma the goddess works closely with the goddess Venus in her aspect of *Venus Felix*, the bringer of happiness and good fortune. Thus, the Temple of Venus and Roma at the Colosseum embodies the city and its good fortune across Rome's far-flung empire. Venus is the goddess of love (*amor* in Latin), and the Romans have noted that Roma and Amor spell each other backwards.

As might be expected of something representing the might and power of Rome's empire, this double temple is the largest in Rome,

outdoing even the Temple of Jupiter on the Capitoline Hill in size, if not in magnificence. (Building space on the Capitoline is extremely limited.) The Temple of Venus and Roma was designed by a skilled polymath, an architect called Hadrian, who between AD 117 and 138 also ran the Roman empire as a side hustle between architectural projects. (The Pantheon in the Campus Martius is another of his works.) With the Temple of Venus and Roma, Hadrian worked with an engineer called Apollodorus of Damascus whom Hadrian allegedly put to death as a result of creative differences over the construction.

The temple was dedicated in AD 135 and each goddess was given a separate sacred room (the *cella*) with the two rooms placed back-to-back to make a single long rectangular building. This stands on an enormous base, 14,500 square metres, approached through a colonnade of grey Egyptian marble. There is a rise in the ground here forming a ridge called the Velia between the Colosseum and the forum. The base is dug into this ridge so that the Colosseum side is higher than the Forum side and has flights of steps leading to the temple proper. (In part because Roman temples are built on civic land prone to flooding, few Roman temples are without steps onto a platform that puts the building higher than predicted water levels.)

There's an impressive array of statuary in and around the temple(s), including those around an altar where newly-wed couples sacrifice for a felicitous union. There's another statue of the she-wolf suckling Romulus and Remus and others of various deified emperors and another of the war god Mars.

The building itself is entirely faced in marble and the tiles of the roof are gilded for a lustrous golden sheen. The whole thing is surrounded by a large *peribolus*, a wall that demarcates the boundary between the sacred ground of the temple and the profane land beyond. (A cynic might note that this temple is also a sanctuary, and a large wall surrounding it makes it easier to vet and exclude any undesirables seeking refuge within.)

Arch of Constantine

Beside the temple and along the route over the Velia to the forum stands the most recent addition to the area, the Arch of Constantine, which was completed relatively recently in AD 315. Those who complain that standards have fallen in Rome since the glory days of 200 years past can point to the arch as an example of what they mean. Other triumphal arches and columns – and there are plenty of them splashed around the city – celebrate the victory of Roman arms over foreign enemies. The Arch of Constantine celebrates Constantine's victory in civil war over the (arguably more legitimate) Roman Emperor Maxentius. Although the alleged excuse for the arch is to celebrate the benefits of Constantine's rule, no one believes this for a moment – not least because construction began long before any such benefits became apparent.

The dedicatory inscription also rather removes any doubt:

> *To Emperor Caesar Flavius Constantine, the greatest, pious, felicitous Augustus, SPQR* [the Senate and People of Rome] *have dedicated this arch with triumphal insignia* [albeit taken from other triumphs, such as Trajan's] *because through his greatness of mind, divine guidance and the* [dubious] *justice of his cause, through force of arms he overthrew the tyrant and his faction.*

The arch itself is somewhat botched together. The basic structure looks as though it was constructed over a forgotten earlier monument on the site and most of the bas-reliefs are taken from earlier monuments from the time of Marcus Aurelius and Trajan. A close look at images of the triumphant Constantine shows that where his head has on occasion replaced that of an earlier character (Hadrian or Domitian), the sculptor has made little effort to reconcile the different style of Constantine's fourth-century portrait with the earlier style of the body beneath.

Gone are the subtleties of second-century sculpture. Where original panels decorate the arch, the images are disproportionate and – in contrast to the natural flow of earlier statuary – the positions of the protagonists seem forced and artificial. One kindly interpretation would be that the different styles of stonemasonry on the arch are a deliberate attempt to reflect both contemporary sculpture and continuity with the past. A less charitable observer might remark that early fourth-century Rome simply does not have enough decent sculptors to adorn the arch properly within the time frame required and, therefore, the city fathers simply looted and repurposed the efforts of a more organized era.

Nevertheless, the arch is an imposing and oddly graceful monument. It's the largest Roman arch for a start, standing a formidable 21 metres high and with not one, but three well-proportioned arches beneath its plinth, covering in total a width of 25 metres. The stonework is marble of different types, although one has to wonder at the statues of barbarian prisoners: they're clearly Dacians and appropriated from a monument of Trajan who fought those people while Constantine did not. The columns on the arch come from a monument of the Flavian dynasty, which probably stood near the amphitheatre and which the ghost of Vespasian would probably like put back.

One of the more interesting aspects of the arch is not what it depicts – which is basically Roman triumphal stonework over the past 300 years – but what it does not. Rome's Christians make much of Constantine's embrace of Christianity (although he was only baptised on his deathbed) and claim that their God provided the 'divine guidance' mentioned in the dedicatory inscription. Yet, if the Almighty did inspire the troops of Constantine to victory over Maxentius, there is little else on the arch that gives credit where it is due. The statuary, motifs and occasional depictions of divinities are all solidly in line with Rome's earlier, non-Christian tradition. For example, Nike – the pagan embodiment of victory – makes a predictable appearance at several points. Overall, the arch is perhaps more symbolic of Rome than its creators would wish. It is huge and impressive, yet relies too heavily on the glories of Rome's past to give beholders great faith in Rome's future.

The Domus Aurea

After contemplating the Arch of Constantine and Temple of Venus and Roma, turn and look over the rest of the Colosseum plaza. The area of the Colosseum gained its name through upheavals during and just after the reign of the Emperor Nero in the mid-first century AD. Nero considered himself an artist with a terribly sensitive disposition. As such, he felt himself creatively crippled by the constrained

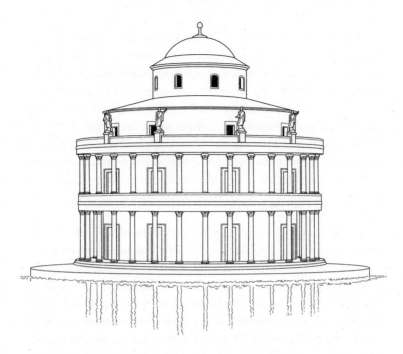

circumstances of the imperial palace he had inherited on the Palatine Hill. He needed somewhere that he could 'live like a human being'. A huge fire that swept through Rome in AD 64 presented Nero with that opportunity.

What a 'human being' needed to live turned out to be a decadently opulent complex of buildings and landscaped parks sprawling over 2.5 square kilometres right in the centre of Rome, complete with a large artificial lake and a massive statue of Nero looking down from the Velia at the entire display. This bronze statue stood just over 100 Roman feet tall (30 metres). The palace was called the Domus Aurea (the 'Golden House') because of the extensive use of gold leaf upon every available surface that was not covered by mosaics or frescoes.

Not much remains of Nero's folly because this example of imperial extravagance left the Roman people deeply aggrieved and resentful, and when Nero was forcibly removed from power, his Domus Aurea went down with him.

Some parts of the Golden House were simply buried by Nero's embarrassed imperial successors who took care to first strip out the valuables. Others – the parts that one can wander through in today's walk – were converted into public buildings. Even Nero's colossal statue was converted. The Emperor Vespasian added a radiate corona to the statue and re-christened it as the image of the sun god Helios. As a landmark, this statue is so distinctive that the entire public space that the Domus Aurea once occupied is now named after it: the Colosseum.

The Flavian Amphitheatre (Colosseum)

Take a while to enjoy the open plaza that this part of Nero's Golden House has become. The centrepiece is a 17-metre-tall fountain called the Meta Sudans (the 'sweating post') because rather than jetting out, water gently oozes down the sides into an ornamental reflecting pool. There's also a very large signpost here with the distances marked to significant places across the empire. This would suggest that if all roads lead to Rome, this signpost shows that they have arrived. (However, the exact distance of all roads to Rome is measured from further west, at the top end of the forum.) After studying the rest of the area, only now turn your attention to the elephant in the room, or rather the gigantic amphitheatre in the plaza. It's impossible to ignore: the arena that Vespasian and his son Titus erected on the site once they had drained Nero's former ornamental lake.

The Amphitheatrum Flavium so dominates this space that later generations will transfer the name of the Colosseum from the entire area to the one building. Twenty-five thousand square metres of it (about six acres) consisting of several million cubic feet of stone standing almost 50 metres high. The massive building is also a sizeable political statement. The Emperor Vespasian was eager to show that stability had returned to Rome after the dysfunction of Nero's reign and the chaos that had followed his death.

Much of the more brutal labour was supplied by prisoners from Vespasian's recent Jewish war, but skilled artisans and free labourers were also employed. In fact, this was partly the point.

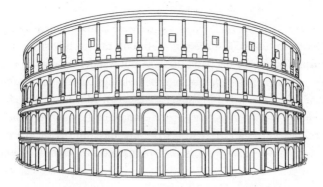

He presented eminent poets with substantial benefits and also rewarded artists such as the restorer of the [statue of] Venus of Cos and of the [remodelled] Colossus. When a mechanical engineer promised to transport some heavy columns at a very low price, he handsomely recompensed the man for his invention, but refused to make use of it. 'You must let me feed the working poor', he said.

Suetonius, *Life of Vespasian* (9 & 18)

The Colossus now stands beside the amphitheatre because Hadrian later moved it there when he built his Temple of Venus and Roma on the Velian ridge. According to one writer (Spartianus, *Hadrian* [19]), a team of twenty-eight elephants was used to effect the transfer that now makes the amphitheatre all the more imposing – the statue seems almost to be guiding visitors inside.

There's room for plenty of visitors – some 50,000 can fit comfortably inside, although the Roman tolerance for crowds means that the building can accommodate 70,000 at a pinch. For a building dedicated almost entirely to the bloody business of death as entertainment, the amphitheatre is itself a remarkably elegant construction. Take a gentle stroll around the perimeter and note the dozens of entrances to the building: eighty of them, with two solely for the use of the emperor himself. Two other entrances are reserved for staff and participants at the 'games', leaving seventy-six entrances available to the general public.

The Imperial Gladiator

No emperor was more devoted to the amphitheatre than the miserable Commodus (AD 177–92) who is a leading contender for the title of Rome's worst emperor ever. Commodus liked to do his killing personally and this eyewitness account by the senator Cassius Dio gives some idea of the proceedings.

On the other days he descended to the arena from the imperial box and cut down all the domestic animals that approached him and others that were brought to him and others in nets. In this way he also killed a tiger, a hippopotamus, and an elephant. After these heroics he retired for lunch after which he decided to fight as a gladiator ... he held the shield in his right hand and the wooden sword in his left, as he took great pride in the fact that he was left-handed. His opponent would be some athlete or perchance a gladiator armed with a stick [the duel was evidently not to the death].

Cassius Dio, *History* (71.19)

The design within is so carefully arranged that the entire building can empty without fuss within half an hour of a show ending. Participants such as gladiators enter through one of the arches reserved for their use, the *Porta Triumphalis* (Door of Victory), but dread leaving through the other, the *Porta Libitinaria* (Door of Death). This arch is named after the goddess of funerals and is used by those making a very final exit after a messy death on the sands.

These arches are reflected in a series of alcoves above and a cunning visual trick has been employed to make the building seem even taller than it is. The entry archways are five paces wide (4.2m), but the corresponding alcoves above are the same width but shorter (6.45 metres to 7.05). This exactly mimics the foreshortening effect that one gets when looking at a taller structure from below and so makes the structure seem even more impressive.

Step inside and walk the cavernous galleries that lead to the stone benches, noting that the Vestal Virgins of Rome get front seats from which to view the action. If there are gladiators or beast fighters practising in the arena, take a walk to the upper gallery (called the *summa cavea* – the only place from which women who are not Vestals can observe the games), which was added by Vespasian's son Domitian. The oval design of the amphitheatre means that even from this most distant of views, the action below seems remarkably close and shockingly intimate.

It's not hard to imagine this place packed with spectators yelling for more blood to be added to that already splashed on the sands below, or the agonized deaths of the tens of thousands of humans and animals that perished here since the building was constructed. Not for nothing has the arena below been called 'the most bloodstained place on earth' – more than 9,000 animals and dozens of humans perished just in the inaugural games when the Emperor Titus formally opened the amphitheatre and the pace hardly slackened over the following centuries. (More recently, the fervent protests of Rome's large and growing Christian community have somewhat reduced the bloodbath, but the killing is by no means over.)

It seems odd to contrast the elegance and sophistication of the building with the depravity that happens within. While the amphitheatre looks like a monolithic construction, it is in fact a conglomeration of materials and architectural styles blended into a harmonious whole by skilled architects and designers working over several decades. The finished building is made of travertine stone (naturally), which is used for the pillars and arches. The stone is held in place by hundreds of iron clamps – some 300 tons of metal were used for just this purpose.

Load-bearing walls and the foundations are a mix of concrete and brick, with concrete being the main ingredient in the base. The land upon which the amphitheatre is built is naturally soggy (there was previously a lake here and originally a marsh), but one of the virtues of the Roman concrete used here is that the wetter it gets, the harder it sets. The deep, solid base of this building is literally the foundation that will carry it onwards through the millennia.

Above ground, some external brick walls are faced with marble. There is also decorative tiling on many surfaces. Other surfaces are lime travertine stone, a form of Rome's favourite building material that comes in shiny white so that the upper tiers of the amphitheatre gleam in the sun. The numerous alcoves in the outward-facing upper tiers contain statues by some of Rome's top stonemasons and sculptors.

Each tier of the building is of a different order of architecture. The ground floor is in the muscular Tuscan style while the level above is in the more graceful Ionic order and above that one finds the downright fancy Corinthian style. The entire building is an architectural masterpiece, from the maze of tunnels and subterranean rooms beneath the arena that deliver the reluctant participants to the surface, to the 100 plus drinking fountains placed for the convenience of the spectators, to the conveniences into which full bladders eventually discharge that water.

On some days, those walking by the amphitheatre will observe tall poles being placed into pre-designed slots at the very top level of the building and a maze of rigging extending across the entire structure. The people working here are skilled topmen from the Roman fleet at Misenum. The 'sails' they manipulate are giant sunshades that can be pulled across the top of the amphitheatre to screen the thousands packed into the stands below. These sunshades – called *velaria* – are so often deployed that the sailors have a special barracks and workshop (the Castra Misenatium) situated on grounds near the amphitheatre.

The Ludi

These are not the only support buildings around. The most conspicuous of the remainder are the *ludi*: the schools where Rome's gladiators are trained. However tough you might have considered your schooldays, rest assured that life in the gladiator schools is much, much harder. Gladiators here are Rome's top athletes, finely trained to meet the standards of a very exacting audience. While a top gladiator might only fight in mortal combat once or twice a year, the training is brutal, and a student who flunks might end up as practice fodder to get a more promising candidate accustomed to the business of killing.

Many gladiators are condemned criminals and their *ludus* is also a prison. The biggest of these schools is the appropriately named Ludus Magnus, which is close enough to the Flavian Amphitheatre to be connected by a tunnel. Those interested in seeing some sparring may drop in here to watch the gladiators practise in a small arena with seating provided for spectators. There may be an inordinate number of ladies present, for although women are precluded from getting close to gladiators in the amphitheatre, many like to see these virile sex symbols close up. (Very, very close up, if some of the scandalous rumours are to be believed. In fact, some maintain that the fascination of Commodus with gladiatorial combat is because he was conceived through an illicit affair between a gladiator and the emperor's wife.)

Depending on one's taste in these matters, there are different flavours of gladiator available in each school. The Ludus Dacius specializes in 'Thracian'-style fighters who fight with a shield and a short curved sword, while the smallest of the gladiator schools is the Ludus Gallicus where heavily armoured fighters of the 'Samnite' or 'Murmillones' type are trained.

Those interested in viewing beasts even more exotic might prefer to step into the Ludus Matutinus, which trains 'Venatores' and 'Bestiarii' – fighters who go against animals rather than their fellow humans. Depending on what the far-flung reaches of empire have managed to deliver, there might be giraffes, rhinoceroses, lions, leopards, bears or wolves confined here – a complete zoo of death.

The Portico of Livia

Once you have had your fill of the Colosseum, head north-east towards the Esquiline Hill by way of a narrow road called the Via Selci (some locals still call this by its former name of the Clivus

Suburanus). There's a small, blocky archway here, the Arch of Concord, built by Livia, wife of Augustus. This archway came close to being another victim of Nero's Golden House, the outer reaches of which you are still walking over. Beyond that, up a flight of steps twenty paces wide, is the Portico of Livia. This also was built upon the remains of a lavish private residence – not Nero's megalomaniac scheme but the home of a wealthy aristocrat called Pollio, which foreshadowed both Nero's more ambitious scheme and its replacement with a public utility.

> *To you, Concordia, Livia dedicated a magnificent shrine to be presented to her beloved husband. But let future ages be aware – where Livia's colonnade now stands, there was a huge palace, a single house like a city with a greater area than that encompassed by the walls of many a town.* [A touch of hyperbole here.] *It was levelled to the ground ... because its luxury was deemed harmful. Augustus chose to overthrow this vast structure, destroying the wealth he had inherited.* [Pollio left his estate to Augustus.]
>
> Ovid, *Fasti* (6.636-48)

Allow some time for the portico that now stands upon the site, because this is one of Rome's finest art galleries. 'If you saw the works of art there ... in Livia's Portico, you could easily become oblivious to everything else outside,' remarks the writer Strabo (*Geographia* [5.3.8]). The portico is over 100 metres long with three niches on each side of a row of double columns. The objets d'art are displayed in the rectangular central niche and on the walls of the semi-circular ones on each side.

This is a place of quiet beauty and serenity where often the only sound is that of the fountain splashing in the central square or the murmur of quiet conversation in the semi-circular apse on the south side. 'Vines cast their shade over the portico from pergolas darkening the paths,' remarks Pliny the Elder (*Natural History* [14.11]) who seems to have regarded this as one of his favourite spots in Rome.

Trajan's Baths

To finish today's walk, one does not have to go far – the Baths of Trajan abut right against the portico. While any baths are going to fail in comparison with the downright sybaritic pleasures of yesterday's dip in the Baths of Caracalla, those of Trajan make a sporting effort to keep up. Just within the Servian Wall, the Baths of Trajan provide an excellent substitute bathing spot for those too busy or too idle to avail themselves of Caracalla's more distant offering. The baths also once mirrored, to some degree, the gender arrangements of Caracalla's baths, so that when those baths were open to men only, Trajan's baths were open to women only and vice versa.

The great thing about the Baths of Trajan is the thought that has gone into the design, starting with the orientation of north-east to south-west, which gives the structure maximum shelter from the wind (bearing in mind that the baths are at the foot of the Oppian Hill, which is itself a pretty effective windbreak for winds from that direction), while at the same time getting the best of the afternoon sun.

When Trajan took up the challenge of finishing the baths, he turned the actual execution over to the famed architect Apollodorus – that same architect who himself faced execution when he criticized the temple designs of Hadrian, Trajan's successor. As is usual with baths in Rome, the complex is more than just somewhere to get wet.

Name Those Baths

Technically one should refer to the Baths of Trajan as the Baths of Domitian, for construction was begun by Vespasian's little-favoured younger son. Once again, the foundations rest upon the outer reaches of Nero's sprawling Golden House. The baths were designed with grandiosity in mind from the start, perhaps because of Domitian's sibling rivalry with his imperial predecessor and far more popular older brother Titus, who built a set of baths nearby. It seems that construction stalled upon the assassination of Domitian (who was really unpopular), but when Trajan took up the task a decade later, he had a large canvas to work upon, for Domitian had cleared for construction a space of some 120,000 square metres.

There are massive halls for physical exercise and libraries (in Greek and Latin) for scholarly contemplation. The gardens are liberally dotted with fountains fed from a massive cistern situated slightly higher up the Esquiline Hill than the baths themselves.

THE TWENTY-FIRST CENTURY WALK

This is less of a walk than a ramble around a very narrow area packed with the remnants of one of the most fascinating parts of Rome. Of all walks, this is the one best planned well in advance. In summertime the area is often packed with crowds of tourists and those dedicated to extracting money from them, whether these be official guides offering tours of the Colosseum, vendors of tourist tat, or out-and-out pickpockets. Given the proximity of the sights, you can go from one site to another without selecting a particular direction.

To see the remains of Nero's Golden House, one must be part of an official tour; only small groups are allowed into the structure at any one time. Those parts of Nero's mansion still standing are in pretty good condition, precisely because they were buried by the emperors who came afterwards. The underground conditions protected some of the delicate friezes and paintings from moisture until the buildings were discovered during the Renaissance, when they created a stir among the artistic community in Rome. Soon, artists including Michelangelo and Raphael were lowered underground by rope to see the artwork for themselves.

The result changed the way artists approached their work, but it was also an early example of tourists destroying the very thing they have come to see. Thanks to the imported damp from which they were so long protected, most of these inspiring frescoes are now shadows of their former selves. There are literally hundreds of thousands of square feet of frescoes down there, and embattled curators say it's a race to save them from chemical pollutants, mould and fungus.

It does not help that the area above on the Oppian Hill became a park in later years and tree roots have been infiltrating the underground structure ever since. (One particular culprit is a Himalayan pine tree given to Mussolini by the Japanese in 1921.) Removing the damaging trees is a tricky business, since the roots have infiltrated the mortar and in some cases are all that is holding the brickwork together.

It's a good idea to check what restorations are planned or under way, as the ongoing battle to preserve the site results in frequent closures. Only a few rooms of the 150 or so on the site are currently open to the public, but these are well worth the visit. There are not many places in Rome where one can be assured of walking in the exact place where the infamous Nero himself once trod.

Right where the entrance to Nero's main building formerly stood are now the remains of the Temple of Venus and Roma. This is still a sacred spot because Roma's side of the temple has become the church of St Francesca Romana. Venus' side is considerably more dilapidated. Of the gilded tiles on the roof nothing has been seen for centuries. Nevertheless, this temple has done much better than the nearby shrine of Isis and Serapis, the exact location of which can only be guessed from shattered fragments of stonework scattered around the area. Of the Temple of Venus and Roma, though much is gone, much remains. Were it not for the massive structure of the Colosseum overshadowing everything else nearby, the remnants of Hadrian's temple would be the most spectacular ruins in the area.

One rival for that title is the Arch of Constantine, which is much more accessible than Nero's Domus Aurea, although it's a good idea to pack a pair of binoculars or a camera with a good lens, since the upper parts of the arch will still be at least 20 metres away no matter how closely you approach. (A spiked fence around the base ensures that this is not too close.) If the arch itself is for some inexplicable reason the only purpose of your visit to the area, you can probably find a decent replica much closer to home. This is one of the world's most duplicated arches, so Constantine's architects evidently did something right.

Americans can find their replica by Union Station, Washington DC, and Australians theirs on the Gold Coast. Europeans are spoiled for choice, from the relatively modest Marble Arch in London to the spectacular Arc de Triomphe across the Channel in Paris and the Brandenburg Gate in Berlin. Only serious devotees of imitation arches should attempt to view the Arch of Triumph in Pyongyang, North Korea.

The original arch has cleaned up nicely after centuries of neglect. It was once made part of the family fortifications of one of medieval Rome's many feuding clans. Afterwards, paintings from the early modern era show that it badly needed weeding. Serious restoration work started over 200 years ago with the removal of those houses on either side that had used the arch as a bonus wall, and restoration work has continued right up to the 1990s. The arch lacks some of the elaborate decorations it possessed in its heyday, such as gilded lettering in the inscriptions, but it is once again something that Constantine would be proud to recognize.

The same cannot be said for the Portico of Livia, which has vanished with hardly a trace. This serves as a reminder that those wanting their monuments to be preserved for the ages should work with concrete. Brick is too easily reused, stone monuments become urban quarries for those who think they have better uses for the stone, and bronze gets melted down to become things like cannons. Upon the fall of Rome, the delicate artworks in Livia's portico were quickly stolen or vandalized (literally – the Vandals sacked Rome in AD 533 and took everything of value that could be carried away). Thereafter, the stone and brickwork were quickly recycled.

The Vandals also broke the aqueducts to deprive Rome of water. These aqueducts were never repaired, and with the loss of the aqueducts the Baths of Rome went also. Medieval monks of the Church of St Peter in Chains made a decent sideline selling off marble and brick from Trajan's baths to local stonemasons and burning down the stone for lime to be used in concrete. While not much of the baths survive, the ruins can be compared to an ancient plan of the original building to give an idea of what goes where. The best approach to the baths is through the Parco del Collo Oppio. Expect to be shooed away by irritated security guards if you get too close to the active archaeological excavations ongoing here.

Finally, of course, it's time to visit the Colosseum. Don't bother looking for the colossal bronze statue that once stood alongside it. There remain only traces of what might have been the pediment. The statue remained until the Middle Ages; at least, the Venerable Bede, writing in Britain during the eighth century, assumed it was still standing. If the Colossus was still there in 1349, it would have certainly gone down in the massive earthquake that rocked the city of Rome that year.

That earthquake would have damaged the Colosseum itself a great deal less if the locals had not assiduously salvaged all the iron clamps holding the building together and thereafter mined much of the structural support for building stone. The south side of the Colosseum lost much of its structure in the quake and the popes of Rome enthusiastically pillaged the rubble for their various building projects. Fortunately, in the eighteenth century, Pope Benedict XIV put an end to the destruction by making the Colosseum a sacred site, based on the mistaken belief that large numbers of Christians had been thrown to the lions there. (In fact, most Christians were martyred in the Circus of Nero on the Vatican Hill – Christian victims in the Flavian Amphitheatre were mostly executed there with their beliefs incidental to other offences.)

In 1820, serious restoration work stabilized the remaining structure of the Colosseum, which is today the most visited place in Italy. Most of the arena floor is now gone, allowing visitors to see the maze of rooms and corridors below that were invisible to ancient spectators. The seating remains functional and indeed is still in use, for part of the flooring has been restored so that the Colosseum today is a spectacular venue for (non-lethal) events such as musical or artistic extravaganzas.

REGIO VIII: PART I – THE FORUM ROMANUM

In the Heart of Rome

Today's walk takes us right into the heart of Rome, into the Forum Romanum. This location is as old as the city itself, where the new arrivals under Romulus traded with the Sabines of Titus Tatius who lived on the hills on the other side of the valley. Originally this is where floods from the Tiber ran down to the marsh where the Colosseum now is, and even in the Republican era there were times when this walk could only have been done as a paddle in a small boat.

As with most Roman cities the forum in Rome itself is the beating heart of town, a bustling, busy throng of humanity who swarm the roads and side streets. Most are occupied with shopping, socializing or business, and pay little attention to the buildings and monuments all around them that are part of their everyday experience. Yet here you are in the most ancient, hallowed part of the Roman empire. All around you memories have become history that has faded into legend as century after century has rolled by.

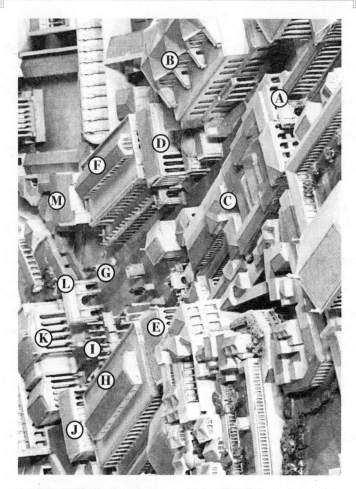

A ARCH OF TITUS

B BASILICA OF CONSTANTINE

C THE SHRINE OF VESTA

D TEMPLE OF ANTONINUS AND
FAUSTINA

E TEMPLE OF CASTOR AND
POLLUX

F BASILICA OF AEMILIUS

G LAPIS NIGER

H JULIAN BASILICA

I ROSTRA

J TEMPLE OF SATURN

K TEMPLE OF CONCORD

L ARCH OF SEVERUS

M SENATE HOUSE

The Sacra Via

Start on the road towards the forum with your back to the Arch of Constantine and your face towards the Arch of Titus. You are standing on Rome's Main Street, the Sacra Via. Unless you have chosen to stand here at the dead of night, you'll be jostled by the crowd that constantly passes back and forth between the Forum Romanum and the Colosseum area.

Since you are standing still and not elbowing your way purposefully through the throng, you are evidently a tourist. As a result, you'll also be surrounded by your own private throng of people trying to sell you something. (There are some things that never change.) Given the mass of traffic on this road, it is just as well that this is one of the widest streets in Rome. It's almost 30 metres wide at this point, with a handsome colonnade on each side and some of Rome's most prestigious shops behind that.

The Sacra Via (the name means 'Sacred Road', so try to ignore the many prostitutes lining the roadside who rather contradict this idea) stretches all the way through the forum. The official terminus of the road is at another very ancient site called the Regia, where we shall arrive in due course. However, while the name stops at the Regia, the actual street continues all the way to the temples on the Capitoline Hill.

For time immemorial this street has been the route taken to the Capitoline Hill by Roman generals celebrating a formal triumph over the enemies of the city. Over the centuries dozens of distinguished Romans (and a few mediocrities) have marched down this street proudly displaying the booty and prisoners captured on campaign while the crowd cheered from the sidelines.

The Sacra Via once used to wend its way from our starting point northwards along the ridge of the Velia, around where the Temple of Venus and Roma now stands (in fact some parts of the former road are still embedded in that temple's foundation), and then on into the forum through the site currently occupied by the Basilica of Maxentius. After the Great Fire of Rome in AD 64, Nero had the road straightened and widened (one of his few sensible acts) so it now runs straight from Colosseum to Capitoline.

This is also probably the oldest street in Rome. One sign of its antiquity is that the name is almost always rendered in the archaic 'Sacra Via' instead of 'Via Sacra' as has been the fashion for more modern streets over the past thousand years. Even here at the start of the street, there's a lot to see. You are right beside the Temple of the Lares built by Augustus in the first century. The *Lares* are often considered as Roman household gods, which is why people talk of 'returning to the *Lares*' as another way of saying 'going home'. However, some *Lares* have a wider brief, which can include the protection of ports or entire cities. From their temple's position at the highest point along the Sacra Via proper, one can guess that these *Lares* have the protection of Rome's most storied road in their charge.

Another temple constructed by Augustus is the Temple of the di Penates, which also stood on the Velia a little further up the street. This fell victim to the building plans of later emperors, but much of the building is now incorporated into the Temple of Peace that now stands at or near the lost site.

Here at the start of the Sacra Via is also a monumental statue and precinct dedicated to Jupiter Stator – 'Jupiter the Stayer'. We are now in the very heart of Rome, for somewhere here was the Porta

The Triumphs of Publius Ventidius

Ventidius is an interesting character because he went along the Sacra Via in not one but two triumphs during Rome's late Republican era. In the first, he was a child taken captive during the Roman campaign to capture Picenum in northern Italy. In his second parade down the Sacra Via, Ventidius was the triumphing general celebrating victories that he had won commanding Roman legions on the eastern frontier – an extraordinary tribute to Rome's openness to men of talent.

Mugonia, one of the gates in the wall built by Romulus to defend the Palatine Hill some time back around 750 BC. At the time, Romulus was battling the Sabines who lived on the Viminal Hill across the valley where the forum now stands. The Sabines were understandably upset that the Romans had kidnapped their daughters during the infamous Rape of the Sabines and were literally after blood. The Romans were losing and backing up the Velia towards the Mungonia Gate. With a rout imminent, Romulus prayed to Jupiter to hold the line and vowed a temple to the god on that spot if the Romans managed to hold. They did, and that temple – extensively remodelled and rebuilt – is still here.

Abutting this temple is the house owned by Julius Caesar whence he departed on the Ides of March for his fateful rendezvous with the senate in the temple area to the north of the forum. For now, it's time to start walking towards the large traffic-calming obstacle that stands in the middle of the road right on the summit of the Velia. This obstacle is known as the Arch of Titus.

The Arch of Titus

Titus was the older son of the Emperor Vespasian. While his short reign is fondly remembered by the Romans, the Jewish people have a much lower opinion of the man. A look at the bas-reliefs within the archway give the reason why. Piled upon the carts depicted here are unmistakably Jewish icons such as the seven-branched candlestick called the Menorah. This arch, in fact, celebrates the victory of the Roman legions led by Titus over the Jews in their rebellion of AD 66. Thanks to the stubborn defenders of Masada, this war went on until AD 73 but was effectively over by AD 71 when Titus celebrated his victory with his triumphal parade up this very street.

Titus himself did not live long enough to see the arch erected. He died young, victim of a brain tumour or – as die-hard Jewish rebels firmly believed – divine vengeance. The arch was his younger brother Domitian's attempt to gain reflected popularity by showing devotion to his deceased brother's memory.

A memorial arch would not be an arch were it not an impressive mass of masonry, and this arch stands well in comparison to Constantine's larger but more slipshod effort further along the Velia. Titus' arch is 15.5 metres tall and just over 13 metres at the base. Most of this base is empty space beneath an eight-metre-wide arch that stretches to about half the height of the overall monument. (The Romans like to leave a lot of space at the top of an arch for inscriptions that tell passers-by what the thing is all about.)

In the case of this arch, the designers decided to let the pictures do the talking. The inscription itself, although gilded in precious metal, is almost laconic in its brevity:

> *From SPQR* [the Senate and People of Rome] *to the deified Titus Augustus, son of the deified Vespasian Augustus.*

Step under the arch to see the pictures that go with this caption. They are bas-reliefs carved with a fluid artistry that nevertheless accurately depicts the subjects: the participants in Titus' triumphal parade. On the upper arch there is, naturally enough, a depiction of Victory who presides over the scene below where a cart laden with treasure stands against a blue background. The golden objects on the cart are deeply engraved and painted with yellow ochre.

The other panel to the right shows Titus in his triumph. While a triumphing general rode along to the adulation of the crowd, a slave held a laurel wreath over his head but also had the job of whispering in the general's ear: 'Remember, you are just a mortal man.' Titus, in his sculpture, has the slave replaced by the goddess Victory, while the embodiment of Valour drives the horses. What Victory might have whispered is a matter for speculation. If you can't get enough of Titus and sculptural displays of military prowess, go directly to the Circus Maximus. The senate evidently decided that if one arch is great, two must be even greater and therefore erected a supplementary arch to Titus at this site.

Otherwise, it is time to follow the Sacra Via down the Velia into the forum, an intimidating complex of towering buildings, temples and basilicas that is swarming with tradesmen, businessmen, politicians, hucksters, tourists, shoppers and the inevitable prostitutes.

The Bankers' Bench

You will note that some businessmen have set up shop right against the temple pediments, which are usually quite a bit taller than head height. These businessmen are there because they are bankers dealing in cash and they really appreciate having a solid wall at their backs. In front of each man is a bench (*banca*), which gives the profession its name. Those coming from foreign parts need to exchange their money for something acceptable to Roman tradesmen and the bankers provide this service with the various currencies stacked on their benches. They will also cash in letters of credit supplied by their counterparts in faraway cities, thus saving travellers from making their perilous journey with tempting amounts of ready cash on their persons.

The Basilica of Constantine and Maxentius

One can make a case that the more an emperor is worried that his legitimacy may be challenged, the bigger the monument he feels compelled to build and the closer to the forum he builds it. Augustus, who had not only to establish his legitimacy but also that of the Principate generally, was a great builder. Another example is the Flavian Amphitheatre, built by Vespasian, the first non-Julio-Claudian emperor, and yet another is the Arch of Constantine, built by the emperor who overthrew Maxentius. (A possible exception is Hadrian, who quashed challengers early in his reign but seems to have simply liked building things.) And then we have the Basilica of Maxentius, built by the emperor who was successfully challenged by Constantine.

If we go by this theory, then Maxentius was (rightly) very worried indeed about his position. Not only is his eponymous basilica forum-adjacent, it is actually within the forum and is the largest building there. It is possible that Augustus' Temple of the di Penates was sacrificed to make way for this basilica, in which case the death of Maxentius shows that impressing the populace is not worth the price of offending gods, however minor you think they may be.

Once Constantine had disposed of Maxentius, he completed the basilica – not least because he also had a few issues with the legitimacy of his reign. If size helped legitimacy, Constantine was on to a winner. Maxentius designed his basilica to sit on a concrete platform of 100 metres by 65, which meant that not only the Temple of the di Penates had to go, but also a small park established by Domitian. The building has three massive naves, each many times higher than any practical reason might call for. (The design appears to have been lifted from that necessitating large halls, namely those housing the Roman baths.) The load-bearing walls are correspondingly solid, with some being 6 metres thick at the base. The interior has wide aisles between the naves and a positive forest of pillars and columns leading from the east-facing frontage designed by Maxentius. Another small copse of columns lines the steps from the street to this entrance to the basilica itself.

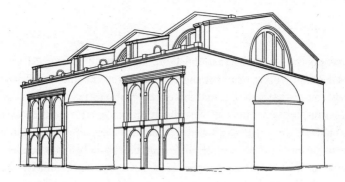

Constantine wanted to make sure that the people of Rome considered this *his* basilica, so he rather ruined the original elegance of the design by adding another entrance, this one directly from the Sacra Via. Anyone entering from here could get a good look at their new emperor, as personified by a gigantic statue in the apse. The building was roofed with an array of bronze tiles, making the overall structure one of the largest and most original monuments in the entire city – no wonder, then, that Constantine wanted to expropriate the credit for it.

The *Forma Urbis*

The back wall of the Temple of Peace has simply the best mural on the back of any temple anywhere. It's a marble map of Rome, known as the *forma urbis*. It shows as much of the city of Rome as could be carved at a scale of 1:250 on to a slab of marble 234 metres square. The map is both accurate and very detailed. Columns, stairways and seats in the theatre are all there in painstaking detail, with each location carefully labelled. Regrettably the plan is almost two centuries old, so for example the basilica of Maxentius/Constantine is not there, but it's still a remarkable feat of cartography.

The name 'basilica' is from Greek and means literally 'the king's porch': the place where the king would sit in judgement while official business was conducted around him. These days, basilicas have all sorts of functions, from religious to domestic to military, but the basilica of Maxentius, er … of Constantine, stays true to the original civic purpose. As well as its chief function of impressing the sandals off anyone entering, the basilica holds a small army of clerks and even the emperor, if he is around, might sit in judgement beneath Constantine's statue on the apse.

Temple of Antoninus and Faustina

The next temple is of interest because it is the only edifice in the forum that is dedicated to the memory of a woman. This is the temple constructed by the uxorious Emperor Antoninus Pius (AD 138–61), the man under whose administration the Roman empire is reckoned to have reached the apogee of its power. Sadly, Antoninus' beloved wife Faustina did not live long enough to enjoy much of her husband's long and peaceful reign. She died in AD 140 and Antoninus immediately set about planning her memorial.

The result was a tidy and well-built temple in the Corinthian style, adorned with gleaming white marble facing and a frieze of elaborate bas-reliefs. Within this building a statue of Faustina occupies the *cella*, where normally a statue of a god or goddess might be. Since the *cella* is closed off from the general public, a large statue of Faustina is also placed outside the temple to keep her memory fresh in people's minds.

After the death of Antoninus, who surpassed the traditional threescore years and ten by another five years, the senate decided that he should be immortalized within the same temple that he had built for his wife. This was a sweetly sentimental idea that had the practical advantage of saving the cash that would need to be spent on a separate memorial. So, statues of Antoninus have duly joined his wife's both in the *cella* and outside, and the state paid for the additional inscription: 'To the divine Antoninus and Faustina, by order of the Senate.'

Interlude

As you are by now a veteran visitor to the sights of Rome, you will have remembered to bring along the necessary for your mid-morning break: namely a cup, a plate and a napkin. Perhaps because of bitter experience, Roman pavement eateries do not supply these but instead expect customers to bring their own. (In fact, even those invited to dinner with the emperor are expected to bring their own napkins.)

So, properly equipped, stop at one of the many food carts along the Sacra Via and enjoy some *posca et moretum* for a traditional Roman snack. You don't want to be seen eating such low-class fare within residential premises and, in any case, the *moretum* – a bright green spread that you slather upon fresh-baked bread – contains enough garlic to curl the hair of anyone within ten feet indoors. But *moretum* is remarkably tasty and pairs well with the *posca*, a soldier's drink mixed from wine, water and vinegar. *Posca* is also remarkably effective at killing thirst, something necessary in the close and sweaty confines of the forum.

While consuming the snack, enjoy the passing parade and the bustling scene. Although everyone, including the Romans, thinks of Romans as 'the people of the toga', the only togate individuals you'll see are those with official business within the basilicas, where formal dress is required. Almost everyone else wears a tunic. The most basic tunic is simply a sort of tube with holes for the head and arms at the top and a belt around halfway down. However, there are tunics and *tunics*. Those wearing tunics of unbleached wool are probably slaves, while other tunics might be of fine Egyptian linen, and you can make a fair guess as to the wealth of the wearer by the expense of the dye used to colour the garment. Almost every colour of the rainbow can be produced from the right vegetables. Be sure, though, to leap to attention if the garment is completely purple. The only person allowed to wear that is the emperor.

Working-class women and unmarried girls also wear tunics, but respectable married women are immediately obvious from their tunic-wearing slaves and distinctive *stola*: a dress often accompanied by an oversized scarf/shawl called a *palla*. Since the only flesh visible is the face (which is sometimes veiled), one might call such dress modest, if not for the fact that the cut and fabric are generally as rich as the family budget can bear. In Rome, appearances matter.

The Regia and the Shrine of Vesta

One group of respectable but definitely unmarried women who generally wear a *stola* are the Vestal Virgins of Rome. That's their home and shrine just ahead to the left, with the Regia in front, abutting the outer wall. At the Regia we are again in ancient ancient Rome. This building is relatively modest because the original construction was by Numa, the second king of Rome, whose idea of an impressive palace included new straw on the thatch of his hut.

The Sacred Fire

At the apex of the conical roof of the Vestal shrine, there's an aperture for smoke to escape from the *cella*, which is right in the heart of the Vestal complex. Where there's smoke, there's fire, and in this case that's good news because it presages disaster for Rome if the sacred fire is ever allowed to go out. It's certainly a terrible omen for the offending Virgin who failed in her duty of tending the fire. She can expect a sound whipping from the Pontifex Maximus who needs to immediately rekindle the blaze through a tedious ritual accompanied by several exculpatory sacrifices.

The Regia is now something of a relic, and there's uncertainty as to whether in the Republic the 'regal' person within was the Rex Sacrorum or the Pontifex Maximus. Both of these persons held high religious office and might have used the building as an administrative base. (The presence of sacred objects within precluded the Regia from ever being used as a domestic residence.) The point is now moot, because more recently both these religious offices have been taken over by the emperor and the administration transferred to the Palatine. The Regia remains a small but very elegant building, shaped like an irregular pentagon, and it's worth popping your head around the door to imagine Julius Caesar working at a desk within (he held the rank of Pontifex Maximus until his untimely death). As mentioned previously, the Regia is where the Sacra Via comes to an official end, but the road goes on and our walk shall also.

It's also a terrible omen for Rome if it turns out that a Vestal Virgin isn't. Quite often this is discovered when the wrath of the gods lets people know something is amiss. Pestilence, earthquake or barbarian invasion might cause people to give close and suspicious scrutiny to the social lives of the Vestals or even an invasive check on their virginity. A Virgin who breaks her vows of chastity is nevertheless protected from direct harm. Therefore, no one touches her sacred person as she is carried in a funeral procession to a little room excavated into the walls of Rome. There the unvirginal Vestal is sealed within to spend her last hours in darkness and silence.

It is sacrilege for males even to set foot in the sacred areas of the Vestal shrine – even with the best of motives. When the building

Horror in 114 BC

They say that a certain Vestal, Helvia, was struck by lightning while she was riding. Her horse lay stripped of its harness; and she herself was left near naked, with her garment pulled far up as if on purpose. Her slippers, rings, and head-dress were scattered all around her and her blackened tongue protruded from her mouth. The soothsayers declared that this signified disgraceful misdeeds [had been perpetrated] *by the Vestal Virgins ... The Vestals were duly convicted and punished but to avert disaster signified by this strange and terrible omen ... two Greeks and two Gauls were buried alive on the spot.*

Plutarch, *Roman Questions* (83)

caught fire in 241 BC (a hazard of keeping an open flame always on the premises), the Pontifex Maximus rushed in from the Regia and managed to save the Palladium, one of the most treasured objects in the shrine. The Palladium was a wooden (and therefore flammable) statuette of Athena, which the Romans believed to have been carved by the goddess herself. The statuette played a significant role in the fall of Troy and was allegedly brought to Italy by either Aeneas or the Greek hero Diomedes. As a result of his heroism in saving this priceless sacred artefact, the Gods struck the Pontifex blind. To save the statue he had, after all, broken the taboo of entering the Vestals' quarters and should therefore have been grateful to have got off so lightly.

The Basilica of Aemilius and What's-His-Name-Again?

There is much more to be said of the Shrine of Vesta (one of the oldest buildings in the forum) and many a legend is told about the mysterious lives of the building's denizens. However, there is also much more forum to be explored, so we must reluctantly leave the shrine behind and turn north to look at the storied marble columns of what Pliny the Elder considered one of the three 'finest buildings the world has ever seen' (*Natural History* [36, (24) 102]).

This is the Aemilian Basilica. (Pliny's other two 'finest buildings' are also in Rome and we shall come to them later.) There was originally a row of shops here, dating back to around 500 BC. With the forum being increasingly used for governmental work, in part because of Rome's growing empire, these shops were mown down in 159 BC and replaced by a splendid basilica built by order of the censor Marcus Fulvius Nobilior. Doubtless the censor had hoped that posterity would call this building the Fulvian Basilica.

Then, in 78 BC, one Aemilius Lepidus promoted the role one of his ancestors had played in the basilica's construction and renovated the place, taking care in the process to include family portraits and memorabilia. Successive generations of Aemilians continued to embellish the basilica until it had been almost entirely rebuilt and in the process almost entirely renamed. Today, Romans call this the Basilica Aemilia and only occasionally add a rather embarrassed 'et Fulvia'.

The basilica, built of travertine stone naturally, is just over 90 metres long with commercial and governmental offices sharing different parts of the building. This means that the Basilica Aemilia occupies the entire central frontage of the north side of the Sacra Via from the temple of Faustina and the Senate House. The *tabernae* tucked under the arches offer a wide variety of goods. The building is roofed with wooden tiles. Therefore, the entire enclosed mall makes shopping something of a pleasure if winter gales or summer thunderstorms are raging outside. Although the basilica's *tabernae* are now over half a millennium old, they are still called the 'new shops' because they replaced the 'old shops' that were demolished for the basilica's construction.

The Shrine of Venus Cloacina

Before entering the building, pause at the steps leading up from the forum to consider the small circular shrine to Venus Cloacina. There's a statue of two female figures here. The one holding a flower is Cloacina herself. The flower is presumably strongly scented because the 'Cloacina' aspect of Venus represents Rome's most functional major work of civic engineering. This effort converted the small stream of the Cloacina into the Cloaca Maxima – the giant drain that has dried out the forum marsh, and which now carries the excrement of thousands of Romans into the Tiber.

Marriage Down the Drain

The same aspect of the goddess Venus that represents the Cloaca Maxima sewer also represents the sanctity of sex within marriage. This is not quite the mind-boggling juxtaposition it first seems, for Venus Cloacina is properly called 'Venus the Cleanser' and she is closely associated with the Sabine King Titus Tatius. He made the laws legitimizing marriage between Romans and Sabines. Thus, with the blessing of Venus, Tatius cleansed the stigma of intercourse (of all types) between the two peoples of early Rome.

The Lacus Curtius and the Lapis Niger

Now return to the forum and step over the invisible barrier that separates the commercial from the governmental forum. At one time it was forbidden to enter this end of the forum unless wearing a toga, but in recent times this rule has been relaxed. This is partly for the simple reason that a majority of Romans these days do not even possess a toga, but also because a lot of governmental functions have been transferred to the imperial quarters on the Palatine.

Nevertheless, some high-powered governmental business still happens hereabouts, from the praetor sitting in judgement in the Basilica Iulia to the deliberations taking place in the Senate House on our right. The first order of business, though, will be to study the Lacus Curtius, a monument to Roman self-sacrifice marked by a flat slab surrounded by a protective fence. According to the historian Livy, a Roman called Mettius Curtius hurled himself into a mysterious chasm that appeared here in the forum and by his sacrifice saved Rome from impending disaster.

The biographer Plutarch offers a more prosaic explanation, namely that while Romulus was battling the Sabines, a young Sabine war leader tried to charge the Roman lines at this spot. In these early days no one had yet drained the forum and young Mettius Curtius plunged straight into a bog, got stuck and slowly vanished. The Lacus Curtius marks his burial space.

After contemplating the cryptic memorial to young Mettius Curtius (at least everyone seems sure of his name, if not exactly how he met his fate), move on a few paces to a memorial yet more cryptic. It's a simple white memorial with a paving of black marble around it.

There's a Latin inscription on this memorial that testifies to the age of the Roman state. There's a black stone – the Lapis Niger – underneath the memorial that shields it from damage. The Lapis Niger is sacred, everyone knows that, but exactly why it has been venerated for almost ten centuries is uncertain. The Latin inscription might explain this, were it not that the inscription is written in Latin so old that no one can understand it. One word might be 'rex', the word for 'king'. This is very possible because the stone certainly dates back to the Regnal period in Rome. Now the stone sits in its place in the forum, enigmatic and indecipherable, and it will probably do so for a dozen or more centuries to come.

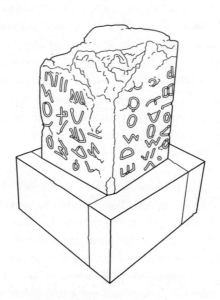

The Republican Legacy

Here also are some monumental sites that are venerable relics of
the Republican era of Rome. With the first, there's nothing to see
but a significantly empty space. It's also a sacred space, a *templum*,
containing statues to Mars Invictus (Mars the Unconquered) and
Romulus. The entire space forms a wide shallow bowl over forty
paces across, which has been the site of some of the most dramatic
moments in Roman history. This is the *Comitium* where the Roman
people met to pass laws – despite a popular misconception, the senate
could not do this and only ratified laws once passed. Rome's greatest
orators and statesmen have stood at this very spot and debated the
measures that changed the course of history.

More particularly the orators stood on a victory monument
originally made of the rams of ships destroyed in the Punic Wars of the
third century BC. This gave the speakers a suitably elevated platform
from which to address the crowd in the *Comitium*, and the ships' rams
(*rostra*) have given their name to thousands of rostrums in later ages.

In fact, Rome owes its existence in a way to the *Comitium*. In the
earliest days of the Republic, when the Romans had just defeated the
people of the nearby city of Veii, the senate was debating whether the
Romans should move to the more elegant and commodious premises
of their new conquest or remain on Rome's somewhat squalid and
unhealthy site. The matter was in the balance until a centurion
stopped with some troops at the *Comitium* and loudly announced:
'Set up the standards. We're staying here.' The senators heard these
words, accepted the omen and Rome remained where it is (Livy, *Ab
Urbe Condida* [5.55]).

Now look across the *Comitium* to the Temple of Concord – there's
a statue in the way of the view. This statue is dedicated to the memory
of Tiberius Gracchus, a reforming tribune who was slain near here
while addressing the people. The younger brother of Tiberius, Gaius
Gracchus, continued his brother's work despite the obstinate and
at times fanatical opposition of the senatorial elite. Eventually the
disagreement ended in violence and the senate, which never hesitated

to use force when its interest was at stake, conducted a brutal purge that cost the lives of Gaius Gracchus and thousands of his supporters.

The consul who led this purge was one Opimius, who then rebuilt an ancient temple in the north-west corner of the forum. This was the Temple of Concord, although the Roman plebs thought that a rededication to the goddess Hypocritia might have been in order.

> *What infuriated the people more than anything else was the erection of a temple of Concord by Opimius. They felt that he was exultantly celebrating a sort of triumph for having slaughtered his fellow citizens. For this reason one night someone carved beneath the inscription the words 'A deed of mad discord has produced this temple of Concord'.*
>
> Plutarch, *Life of C. Gracchus* (17)

To add insult to injury, the senate thereafter made a point of sometimes meeting in this temple. The Gods seem to have disapproved. The Emperor Tiberius had to extensively repair the temple, which was damaged again by a later fire.

It's well worth visiting the temple, even though it may be the legacy of the bloodthirsty Opimius (who Plutarch assures us died 'hated and despised by all'). The Emperor Tiberius installed a famous statue of Vesta within and this started a trend of stashing great works of art on the premises. There are now over a dozen statues and paintings by the most famed artists of past eras and many minor works besides. The elegant, marble-clad facade further emphasizes the dichotomy between the bloodstained past and the present beauty.

The Senate House

Just to the north at the top corner of the forum is the Senate House (often called 'the Curia Julia'). This is where the Roman senate most often meets, although it certainly does not have to. The senate can meet in any temple, and often does if for some reason the Curia is unsuitable. For example, generals on campaign are not allowed within the Roman *pomerium* and kings of any kind are not allowed there under any circumstances, so the senate meets such persons in temples outside the sacred area.

Although the somewhat austere concrete-faced building in the forum is called the Curia Julia, there has been a *curia* there since the Regnal period. (*Curia* simply means 'meeting house'.) Because this building is closely identified with the senate, and the Roman proletariat sometimes strongly disagree with the senate, a lot of rebuilding has been required. For example, the people burned down the building after the death of the populist tribune Publius Clodius Pulcher and pretty much wrecked it again after the death of Julius Caesar (whose cremation, by some accounts, was speeded along by burning benches from the Curia that were thrown on to the pyre).

Thereafter, the building was renamed in honour of the deceased Julius, although it has been often rebuilt in the current centuries. The present building was restored by the Emperor Diocletian in AD 305. These days the senate has lost most of its ancient power and has largely returned to its original function as the city council of the Roman metropolis itself. Nevertheless, accompanied by their tutors, the younger children of senators still gather at the door to learn from business being conducted within, as they hope to conduct it themselves in later years.

The senate only meets in a temple, so officially the Curia is also a Temple of Victory. A statue of the goddess stands in a dedicated shrine. Popular belief holds that if the statue of Victoria ever goes, Rome's empire will go with her.

The Temple of Castor and the Temple of Saturn

For a reminder of the senate's ancient greatness, look just to the south of the Curia at a space in front of the Temple of Castor and Pollux. This is the *Graecostadium* where once foreign embassies delivered speeches to the senate and the people of Rome, pleading for trade deals or just for the legions to stop beating them up. (Incidentally, if

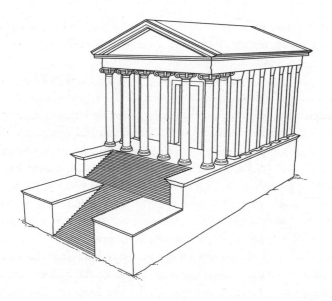

you are interested in jewellery, take a moment to duck off the Sacra Via through the Porta Margaritaria to the little street beyond where Rome's finest gem crafters have set up shop.)

Beyond that is the Temple of Castor and Pollux, usually known – and probably to the annoyance of Pollux, the latter of the divine twins – as the Temple of Castor. There's a pleasant little fountain at the front (the Luturnian Fountain), which marks the spot where the divine twins allegedly appeared in 499 BC to announce Roman victory in a coming battle, which the Romans duly won. The actual temple was built just over a decade later and has been considerably renovated since. It stands on a particularly high pediment because this top corner of the forum was particularly prone to flooding; this, plus its proximity to the *Comitium*, made the temple porch a favoured spot from which politicians would harangue the masses.

It's a large and imposing building, and for that reason the senate often meets there, but it's best admired briefly from the outside before you move along to another large building. And here you will definitely not be allowed within.

This is the Temple of Saturn.

Storing Wealth

Saturn is one of the more cryptic of Rome's gods because he is not exactly a god of the Underworld like the Greek god Hades. Perhaps the best way to describe him is as the God of Death who brings Renewal. He is the dying leaves of autumn that carry the promise of spring buried under the winter snow. He is the grains taken from the mature ears of wheat that will be sown for the next harvest, and the dead and rotting plants that fertilize new growth.

Saturn is the custodian of the Roman treasury, a job that he got partly by accident. Given his role in the Roman pantheon, it is unsurprising that in ancient times the Roman harvest was stored within his temple. A temple has stood here from Rome's earliest times, and indeed the altar in front of the temple was probably here before Rome was. Certainly, the temple pre-dates the time when the Romans were using money, so taxes to the state were paid in grain. When the government started taking coin instead of crops, the temple kept its role but now became a repository of bullion: the *aerarium* (state treasury).

What you see today is the result of very recent renovations after a fire, and while Rome's cash reserves are no longer stored in the basement, the temple still holds the official weights and measures to which all others in the empire must conform.

The Arch of Septimius Severus

We stand now at the base of the Capitoline Hill at the far end of the forum. Many of the sights and wonders are still unexplored, for this is an area so rich in history that it would take weeks to cover it all. (Some future archaeologists are going to take a lifetime.) However, it's time to finish a long day of exploring with one last monument – another triumphal arch. This one has been built right over the *umbilicus urbis* – the spot at which all roads leading to Rome are measured.

Septimius Severus was another of Rome's more underrated emperors, perhaps because he came from North Africa and never lost his unfashionable Punic accent. Nevertheless, this grim (severe?) character was responsible for restoring stability to Rome after a turbulent period of civil war and postponing the horrors of the crises that came close to overthrowing the empire in the decades after his death.

On the other hand, Septimius may have inadvertently been responsible for the series of disasters that almost brought down the Roman empire – and his arch depicts him doing it. The arch is 23 metres of towering travertine, with a stairway conveniently leading to the top where stands a magnificent statue of the emperor in a triumphal chariot accompanied by his two sons. Given the speed with which the arch was built after the triumph of Severus in AD 199, the work can only have been accomplished by teams of sculptors working under one master architect.

As a result, there are small differences in style and composition in the different panels. The theme is consistent though: they show Septimius and his Roman legions kicking the stuffing out of the Parthians. This rival empire had taken advantage of Rome's recent dynastic troubles to raid the empire's eastern frontier, so Septimius' campaign was payback – with considerable interest added.

Carvings of winged Victory flutter around the arch like butterflies, hovering over scenes of successful sieges (of Edessa and Seleucia), conquests (including the sack of the Parthian capital Ctesiphon) and the surrender or submission of various defeated enemies.

The gilded inscription taking up much of the top of the arch reads in part:

> *In the eleventh year of his rule the Senate and the People of Rome dedicate this arch to the imperial Caesar Lucius Septimius Severus Pius Pertinax son of Marcus ... who restored the Republic and the strength and power* (virtus) *of the Roman people at home and abroad.*

The other, and more substantial, part is an elaborate list of the titles, positions and honorary names of the emperor and his sons, since Septimius evidently believed that it enhanced the majesty of his office if it took someone five minutes to read what that office was.

One reason that Septimius was so easily able to beat up the Parthians was that their empire was debilitated by a plague that probably started in Roman Syria and spread east. Rome was just getting over its first brush with that plague (which killed the Emperor Lucius Verus) when the legions of Septimius brought back a mutated and even more virulent strain from the east. At one time this plague was killing 2,000 people a day in the city of Rome alone.

It has been hotly debated how much damage this plague caused. Some argue that the Romans basically shrugged it off, and others that Rome never recovered from the disastrous loss of life and manpower. What is certain is that Rome went into a precipitous decline in the next century and only recently emerged – greatly changed – during the reign of Constantine, whose arch brackets the forum to the east as that of Severus does to the west.

Regrettably, there are no baths in the vicinity, so to relax after a hard day of sightseeing it is necessary to stagger past the forum of Trajan and up the west-facing slope of the Quirinal Hill. Here you will find the luxurious baths of Constantine, where tomorrow's walk begins.

THE TWENTY-FIRST CENTURY WALK

Sadly, those visiting in the twenty-first century are not going to see the Roman Forum. They'll be walking through what in the Middle Ages was called the Campo Vaccino: 'the cow field'. An appalled Roman from several centuries back would have called it a *locus sceleratum* (a crime scene), for the densely packed buildings all crowding upon themselves have disappeared almost entirely. What remains is mostly grass with the occasional lump of marble sitting desolately within.

Our imaginary Roman might indignantly demand to know which barbarians had perpetrated this atrocity. Was it the Huns? The Vandals? The Goths? Sadly, the Roman Forum was not devastated by invaders; the 'barbarians' were the Romans themselves. With the fall of the Western empire, the forum was largely abandoned. Many buildings fell into disrepair and several were destroyed by earthquakes. Not ones to disregard a fine source of stone when there were churches and defences to be constructed, the Romans stripped the wreckage for building material, and when the wreckage was gone they turned their attention to the surviving buildings. These were torn down, the marble recycled to decorate churches and the homes of the wealthy, and the stone burned for lime to make concrete.

Much of the forum ended up rebuilt into the walls of the Basilica of St Peter in the Vatican, so if you want to walk some of the places where the Caesars once trod, you can do it on the Vatican's relocated floors. Pope Nicholas V (1447–55) alone had over 2,000 cartloads of stone transported from the forum and Colosseum to construct the Vatican. Building went on for the next 200 years. The officials in Rome protested bitterly about the demolition of these buildings, and partly as a result we know exactly when some buildings were demolished. The Vestal shrine, for example, went in 1499, and the Temple of Castor and Pollux shortly thereafter, with the order coming directly from Pope Paul III.

To their credit, as the Renaissance went on, the popes went from being vandals (a description that is definitely unkind to the Vandals) to conservators. Much of what has been preserved from the forum is thanks to the efforts of these later pontiffs, and today the Vatican Museums hold a huge treasury of items preserved from the forum and around the ancient city.

With the forum itself, it is easier to document what remains than what was destroyed. The Arch of Titus is still there and in good shape, and the towering naves of the Basilica of Maxentius remain, exposed to the elements, although here much of the damage was caused by an earthquake in AD 841. (Fortunately, Pope Honorius had already saved the bronze roof tiles by transporting them to St Peter's.)

Next to the basilica, the Temple of Antoninus and Faustina stands in remarkably good condition – even enhanced by the addition of a later superstructure. But note the deep gouges on the exterior columns. The story goes that this temple was also scheduled for demolition, but it proved so hard to pull down that it was decided instead to re-dedicate the building as a church.

Apart from a few lonely columns – for example, those of the temples of Saturn and of Castor and Pollux – most of the rest of the forum is gone. The Aemilian basilica is also largely gone – although this really was destroyed by barbarians. Alaric the Visigoth did the deed in AD 410 with a disastrous fire. Green circular stains on the floor of the basilica show where coins dropped by bankers fleeing in haste ended up fused to the pavement by the conflagration. The Curia was so integral to the history of Rome that even the most fanatical of popes were not prepared to sacrifice it to the greater glory of God, and so it remains: a mostly undamaged building standing beside the equally intact Arch of Septimius Severus. The state of preservation of these structures is an evocative reminder of the forum as it could have been today.

However, anyone visiting the forum must stop and visit one hardy survivor that was there before the forum proper was even built and is still there, largely intact, today. The Lapis Niger, so venerated by the ancient Romans, is now carefully preserved under a protective covering. Modern epigraphers, armed with knowledge of prehistoric Latin and Etruscan writing, have made more progress than did the ancient Romans in teasing out the meaning of those cryptic glyphs. The opening lines appear to read, 'No littering or dumping, by order of the King …'

REGIONES VI & V: ROME'S NORTHERN HILLS

Up the Gardens Path

Anyone trying to count the famous seven hills of Rome will struggle somewhat with the counting. For a start, what counts as a hill seems rather random. The Palatine is definitely a hill, and so is the Capitoline. Or do the twin peaks of the Capitoline make it two hills? If the Capitoline is just one hill, then what are we to make of today's walk on the Pincian, the Viminal and the Esquiline, which are clearly protrusions of the same volcanic ridge that runs east to west forming the northern side of the valley of the Tiber?

In fact, Rome does not have seven hills. Or rather, we can use the same poetic licence to say that Rome has five hills, or seven, or nine. The Romans settled on seven because this is a sacred number. That's why we have the Seven Sages, the Seven Deadly Sins, the Seven Wonders of the World and (since we are starting today in a sceptical mood) the Seven Kings of Early Rome. If you are going to have a city that rules the world, it must necessarily stand on seven hills, no matter how far you have to torture geography to obtain that number.

Towards the Pincian Hill

Today's walk starts at the oldest part of Rome or, more particularly, on the part of Rome that was there before the Romans were. This is Sabine country, the home of the people across the valley from the

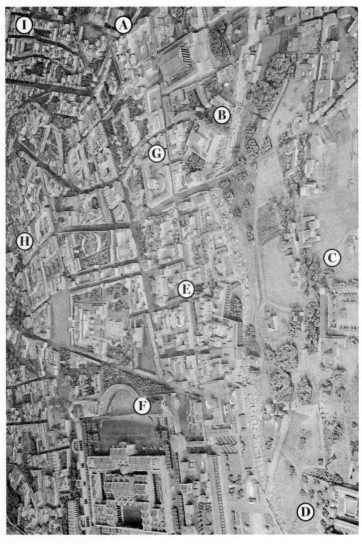

A BATHS OF CONSTANTINE
B CAPITOLINE VETUS
C PINCIAN HILL
D GARDENS OF SALLUST
E BATHS OF DIOCLETIAN
F ALTA SEMITA (VIA SALARIA)
G FLAVIAN SHRINE
H MACELLUM OF LIVIA
I SUBARA

forum who watched in dismay as a horde of settlers from Alba Longa descended on the Palatine and started throwing up defensive walls.

The route leads to the Capitoline Vetus temple on the Quirinal, up the road from the Baths of Constantine where yesterday's walk ended. Unlike the baths built by that Johnny-come-lately, this road celebrated its thousandth birthday quite a while ago. In fact, the name of the road is itself is a clue: Alta Semita means 'the high trail' – the footpath up the hillside. Back in the days when Troy was still a village, people trudged up this hill with sacks of salt to trade with the tribes of the interior. This trade route to the Apennines and beyond is one of the oldest in the world and is named for the principal product carried along it. They call it the Via Salaria, the 'Salt Road', and the Alta Semita is part of that ancient highway within the Roman city walls.

Because Roman religion is way older than Rome, it is possible that those traders stopped to give thanks for a safe crossing of the Tiber at this spot, which has been sacred to Jupiter, Juno and Minerva for time immemorial. The rather nondescript temple here is called the Capitoline Vetus, to distinguish this old Capitoline temple from the 'new' and far better-known temple on the Capitoline Hill.

Why Seven?

To picture the sacred number, imagine a triangle atop a square. The square represents the mundane. It has four sides and is divisible by two, one and four – all the numbers one to four, except the number of sides on the triangle, which make the divine number of three. Three is the number of the Capitoline Triad of Jupiter, Juno and Minerva, and the Chthonic Triad of the Underworld, Pluto, Persephone and Hecate. The idea that three is the perfect number of the divine goes back at least as far as Pythagoras in 500 BC and has been embedded in Western consciousness ever since. Seven, therefore, represents the union of the mundane and divine – a universal and all-encompassing number that is unique because it is also a prime number.

Also somewhere around here is the former home of the (in)famous first-century poet Martial, the elegant Latin of whose verses delighted Romans almost as much as the scatological content appalled them.

> *I live close to the Tiburtine column, near the spot where rustic Flora looks upon ancient Jove. I must climb the Alta ... Semita* [after visiting my patron].

Martial, *Epigrams* (5,22)

Martial's neighbour, 'rustic Flora', deserves another look because this lady certainly fitted with Martial's bohemian lifestyle. Flora is the goddess of flowers and springtime. Every year, the usually rather puritanical Romans celebrate the arrival of spring with the *Floralia*, a festival that includes drunkenly cavorting in public, often wearing no more than a floral garland and a welcoming smile. We shall come to her temple soon, at the spot where it was built over an altar that was already sacred to Flora before the Romans came.

Given the dangers of running about unclad in a city with no police force, it is fortunate for any young ladies in this condition that the Temple of Flora is adjacent to the Temple of Salus (or public safety). Just across from that, and right at our starting point, is the Temple of Quirinus, which is the name bestowed upon Romulus when he became a deity. One might speculate that the temple of Quirinus was placed upon the hill of the Sabines to demonstrate that this hill also was now a part of Rome. Take a moment to wander about this area because, although small, the temples of Salus and Quirinus are known for their exquisite architecture. In a city where even the most enthusiastic tourist eventually succumbs to temple fatigue, these two still should not be omitted.

The Gardens of Sallust

Proceed up the Alta Semita ('The paving is always wet and dirty,' complained Martial) and turn left to leave the old city through the Servian Wall at the Porta Salutaris – after you have had a look at the

Temple of Salus, of course. You'll pass the Temple of Flora on your left as you stop for a quiet moment of contemplation in the Gardens of Sallust. In entering this garden, we pass from the Quirinal to the Pincian Hill, the latter sometimes called the 'Garden Hill', and with good reason. (The Pincian Hill is not one of the traditional seven because it stands outside the Servian city walls.) Here, in a broad arc around the hillside, are the Gardens of Sallust, the Gardens of Lucullus and the Gardens of Pompey.

The Gardens of Sallust once belonged to the historian of that name. Sallust acquired the gardens after the death of Julius Caesar and the land later passed into the possession of the Roman emperors who opened them to the public. These gardens are also something of an outdoor sculpture gallery. Wandering through the park one might come across reproductions of some of the great works of previous eras, such as the statue of the Dying Gaul (one of a group that features several others in different poses) and portrayals of Hermes, Hercules and others. There's even an obelisk purporting to be imported from Egypt.

The Praetorian Barracks

There's no better way to wander up through the outskirts of Rome to the Porta Salaria in the Aurelian Walls. Now turn eastwards towards the Baths of Diocletian and the remains of the praetorian barracks.

Death in the Gardens

The Emperor Nerva died of heart failure in AD 98 while conducting business in the Gardens of Sallust, but most people associate death and the Gardens of Sallust with a more spectacular suicide fifty years previously. This was by a woman who had spectacularly cuckolded her husband. She then compounded the insult by staging a wedding with her lover at a very public and very debauched party. Afterwards, she fled to the gardens to escape retribution. Since her husband was the Roman Emperor Claudius, and since the wife, Messalina, was a serial adulterer, the indignant emperor's retribution was not that easy to escape. Messalina killed herself in these gardens just before Claudius' men could do it for her.

The barracks are largely dismantled today because the praetorian guard has been entirely dismantled. For centuries the allegedly elite force of the praetorians was as much a danger to the emperors as protection for them. The precedent was set early in AD 41 when Caius Caligula was assassinated by officers of the guard, who then went on to see off the Emperor Galba in AD 69. The prefect of the guard was involved in the murder of Domitian in AD 96, and of Commodus a century later. Elagabalus was another victim. Then in the troubles that followed his assassination, the emperors Pertinax, Gordian I and Gordian II were killed by the praetorians.

The low point in the guard's history was probably after the death of Commodus, when the praetorians used their position as the most significant military force in Rome to hold an auction in their barracks, with the empire going to the highest bidder. (The winner, Didius Julianus, was promptly overthrown by Septimius Severus.)

The guard were deeply despised by the Roman people for their overbearing ways, and no one mourned when they were finally disbanded. This was done by Constantine as retribution

for the praetorians' ill-advised decision to side with Maxentius when Constantine marched on Rome. Given their misbehaviour over the preceding centuries, the goddess Nemesis certainly took her time avenging the overweening pride of the praetorians. But as the dismantled barracks demonstrate, she did a thorough job in the end.

Baths of Diocletian

Turning slightly south, follow the arches of the Marcian Aqueduct back towards the Servian Walls to find the Baths of Diocletian. These baths were built at the end of the third century to remediate a long-standing grievance. While the Aventine, Caelian and lower Esquiline hills had public baths of noteworthy size and splendour, the folk of the Viminal had no equivalent, and there was little point in trekking across Rome for a good bath if the return trip left them as dirty and sweaty as when they started out.

The people certainly got their wish because Diocletian's baths are the size of the Baths of Caracalla and, while somewhat less splendid, they have a larger capacity. Thousands of people use the baths at a time, yet the spaces seem relatively uncrowded. This is thanks to clever design whereby the high arches overhead are reinforced by external buttresses, an architectural innovation much used in subsequent decades. The usual gardens and gymnasium enhance the experience of getting wet and clean, but overall these baths lack the sheer exuberance of Trajan's and Caracalla's efforts. The architects have tried hard, but there's the functional feel of a public utility about the place.

At this point you may decide to tack an extra half-hour on to the day by strolling downhill almost back to Constantine's baths to the oddly named Via Ad Malum Punicum (roughly 'Down with the Carthaginians Street'). Here stands a small shrine erected by the Emperor Domitian to mark his birthplace at the former home of his father, the Emperor Vespasian. Domitian also built a grander temple to Vespasian and Titus closer to the Roman Forum, so die-hard fans of the Flavians might want to further extend their walk to view this.

Gardens of Maecenas

Alternatively, follow the Servian Wall along to the Esquiline, noting as you do so that the journey from one 'hill' to the other involves very little uphill and downhill in the transition. We are currently on the outcrop of the ridge known as the Cispian spur. If Rome ever needed eight hills, this could be as easily redefined as a hill as has been the Caelian just to the south.

The Esquiline has always had something of a reputation problem, despite that while Titus Tatius was co-king of early Rome, he moved his residence here to encourage settlement. This was not a great success. It probably did not help that the superstitious Romans knew that an ancient graveyard covered the upper slopes, and during the Republic the bodies of the unburied poor and executed criminals were left on the hillside for scavengers to deal with. The area was also used as something of a rubbish tip by the inhabitants of the other six hills, so residents of the Esquiline tended not to boast about it.

Another attempt to rehabilitate the hill came with the reign of Augustus. The emperor urged one of his most prominent sidekicks, a wealthy patron of the arts called Maecenas, to construct gardens on the upper slopes of the hill. These gardens now run alongside the Servian Wall and that ancient necropolis of ill repute. To some extent the Augustan plan has worked, because the Gardens of Maecenas have turned a more than somewhat unsavoury area into a rather pleasant promenade. The poet Horace – always keen to suck up to his emperor and patron – immediately celebrated in verse this effort at urban renewal.

In the new Gardens of Maecenas slaves once paid to have the
corpses of their companions … brought here in coffins
It was the public burial place for the poor …
Now people live on a healthier hill, and stroll the sunlit ramparts
where once they sadly stared
at a bleak vista of whitened bones.

Horace, *Satires* (1.8)

Pause by the ornamental tower on the grounds of these gardens and from there admire the view of Rome. From this tower in AD 64 Nero watched the Great Fire blaze across his city and (depending whom you believe) either conducted fire-fighting efforts from this location or fiddled about as Rome burned, using the inferno as inspiration to compose on his lyre an impromptu epic on the Fall of Troy.

Again, admire the statuary: these gardens are adorned with sculptures by the famed sculptor Myron, for example, and pause by the auditorium to see if any afternoon concerts are planned. If not, enter the sumptuously decorated building anyway. The partly subterranean structure has superb frescoes and artworks which testify to the impeccable taste of Maecenas, who personally oversaw the construction. Ascend to the side of the building facing south-east for a splendid view of the Alban Hills.

The area called 'the Gardens of Maecenas' is in fact larger than those actual gardens. Adjoining gardens such as the Horti Lamiani and the Horti Calyclani are generally included within the portmanteau description. Continue through these gardens to the Esquiline gate where stands the Esquiline's premier shopping centre: the Macellum of Livia. No one is quite sure whether the wife of Augustus was really involved in building this market, and most of the present structure can be dated to at least a century after her death. However, the place is frequently updated and renovated, so it is quite possible that the original floor plan does go back to Augustan times. The structure takes the form of a large open courtyard with a fountain in the middle and a portico surrounding the space with shops built into the sides. The western side is actually the Servian Wall itself, since the

Romans are always ready to use any handy architecture from earlier eras for their present-day purposes.

The Praeneste Gate (Porta Maggiore)

On leaving the shops, stop to survey the Arch of Gallienus. This arch is much older than the mediocre third-century emperor whom it now commemorates. One of Gallienus' courtiers decided that his emperor needed a commemorative arch in Rome to counterbalance the negative publicity the emperor and his army had been getting from being kicked about by barbarian hordes. The parlous state of the empire meant that neither the treasury nor the courtier had the funds for an arch, so this earlier one was chosen. The former inscription was erased and replaced with the following text:

> *To Gallienus, most merciful of emperors whose unconquered*
> *virtue is surpassed only by his piety and to the most revered*
> *Augusta Salonina* [Gallienus' wife]
> *By Aurelius Victor, a man of great distinction, who in his*
> *total devotion to their protective spirits and majestic …*

Here the grovelling text has been cut off before it expresses anything but blatant untruths. After dealing with a series of rebellions and enemy invasions, Gallienus (ruled AD 253–68) was understandably short-tempered with his opponents, and struggling as he was in the worst of Rome's third-century crisis, he regularly got conquered. His wife was so unrevered that the senate ordered her execution once Gallienus himself was assassinated. As for Aurelius Victor, no other record exists of this most undistinguished gentleman.

The only two reasons for viewing this arch are: firstly, to see if it is as uninspiring as the equally unexciting Arch of Dolabella (it is); and secondly, to pass by it en route to the much more impressive Porta Praenestina in the Aurelian Walls just up the road. The Porta Praenestina, an imposing structure in white travertine stone, is something of an ongoing imperial project. It was started by Claudius as a celebration of two aqueducts (the Aqua Claudia and Aqua Anio Novus) that run in separate channels, one below the other, over the top of the double archway.

Claudius' inscription praising himself for adding these aqueducts is supplemented by later inscription by the Emperor Titus who asserts that his father took charge of restoring these aqueducts and the arch to their former glory. Then, in AD 271, the Emperor Aurelian's builders took advantage of the formerly free-standing structure to build it into the walls of Rome as a gateway, with suitable defensive works added. The final result is worth a visit, even before future emperors decided to add further embellishments. From here the road beneath leads outwards to the ancient city of Praenestina.

Carinae and Subura

Now turn back into Rome and go along the Via Labicana past a rather pretty nymphaeum towards the location of Rome's most infamous 'slum', the Subura. This area has never been as bad as its reputation and, indeed, includes some upper-class housing. The young Julius Caesar lived here. To get there we pass through an area called the Carinae, which is positively respectable. Citizens such as Pompey and Cicero lived there. Even the Emperor Tiberius did for a while. Yet the Carinae is known less for these distinguished personages than for a particularly brutal killing that happened here almost a thousand years ago.

The Baker's Tomb

Also incorporated into the Aurelian Walls is the tomb of Marcus Vergilius Eurysaces built at the end of the first century BC. Marcus was not an emperor, aristocrat or associate of the imperial family. He was a baker and very proud of it. His tomb eschews flights of mythological fancy and is themed around the Roman bakery, with distinctive circular openings on the upper

story and friezes depicting heroic scenes from a baker's life, such as kneading and shaping dough. After all, there's nothing like a struggle with a slow-acting sourdough yeast to really get the blood pumping.

Marcus designed the tomb for himself and his wife, and something of his character shows in the inscription: 'Atistia was my wife, a most excellent lady in life. The mortal remains of her body are in this breadbasket.' This monument celebrates those Romans who struggled from lowly beginnings to make a place for themselves in the big city.

The king who built the Servian Wall, Servius Tullius, was cursed with a daughter, named – as all Roman daughters are – after the father's *gentilicium*. This Tullia married one Tarquinius who matched her in cruelty and ruthlessness. Working on the principle that only one heir was needed in the royal family, the pair quickly dispatched Servius' other daughter and her husband. They then turned their attention to the king himself. By a mixture of bribery and outright intimidation, Tarquinius turned the senate against Servius, and when the king turned up at the senate meeting to defend himself, Tarquinius literally threw him out. After this coup de main, Tarquinius became Rome's next, and last, king – the ill-fated Tarquin the Proud.

The abruptly deposed Servius was heading home when he ran into his daughter. Or, rather, she ran into him – literally, with her chariot. Either at this point or just beforehand the couple's henchmen laid hands on Servius and murdered him, whereupon Tullia completed her journey to her husband by driving her chariot right over the body. The place where this happened is still today called the Vicus Sceleratus, which means literally the 'scene of the crime'.

As to the Subura, the area is now considerably more middle-class than it once was. Most of the population live in large apartment buildings, some of them indeed precariously built and rat-infested, but others solid stone structures 'in which the people of Rome find, without difficulty, excellent housing' (Vitruvius, *De Architectura* [2.8.17]). Take a moment to contemplate a massive wall that separates the Subura from the imperial forums on the other side. This is very literally a firewall between the highly replaceable and flammable buildings of the Subura and the expensive buildings and rare artefacts of the imperial forums that lie on the other side. This wall was also designed, again literally, to keep the Roman poor in their place and prevent the hoi polloi from spilling over into streets occupied by their betters.

The Subura can best be enjoyed by those venturing out with the right company, taking care to avoid dark, twisting alleyways where danger comes not just from muggers lurking in the shadows but also from the contents of chamber pots cheerfully slopped out of upstairs windows. However, the late-night eateries, gambling dens and taverns attract even young aristocratic Romans from more staid parts of the city. In fact, one reason for the Subura's ripe reputation is that the place enjoys a riotous nightlife and nothing brings out the

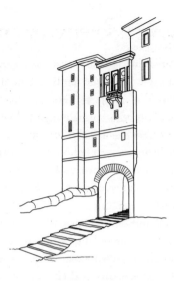

sniffiness of the Roman elite more than the sight of proles enjoying themselves.

Finish the day at the Baths of Titus, just a short walk off to the east. These baths are interesting because they appear to be repurposed parts of the bathing complex in Nero's Golden House. As you splash with your wooden duck in the heated waters of the caldarium, the ghost of Nero may hover over the waters once reserved for himself and his cronies. One clue that these baths were not originally intended for public use is that they lack the large swimming pool of later imperial baths, so the atmosphere here is steamy and rather cosy. One pleasant effect of the design is that the terrace opens to the south, so you can luxuriate in the water while enjoying the late afternoon sunshine and a pleasant vista of the Aventine and Palatine hills.

THE TWENTY-FIRST CENTURY WALK

The twenty-first century walk starts with a stroll north along the Via del Quirinale and Via Venti Settembre, beneath which the most ancient bits of the Alta Semita are thought to lie. The ancient temples of the Quirinal Hill have long gone, but close to where the praetorian barracks once stood is now the headquarters of the Italian Ministry of Defence, which seems somehow appropriate.

The Temple of Flora has vanished and modern Romans have replaced the exuberant lasciviousness of the *Floralia* with the more restrained rites of Pasquale (Easter).

Turn to the left and follow the signs for the US Embassy to find the now somewhat diminished but still beautiful Gardens of Sallust. Expect some locals to eye you askance as you enter, because the gardens are regarded by Romans as 'their' gardens, a place where the cognoscenti find refuge from the madding crowds that swarm the Forum and Colosseum every summer. There are some excellent coffee shops here, and if you arrive after 11am take care to order a cafe macchiato as you enjoy the view of the gardens. Romans don't drink milky coffees except after breakfast, so your choice of drink will show that at least you are not a total tourist.

Many of the monuments from the garden are now elsewhere. The statue of the Dying Gaul is now in the Capitoline Museum, and the Egyptian obelisk (now deemed a Roman imitation of the real thing) now stands at the top of the famous Spanish Steps leading to Bernini's Barcaccia Fountain.

Much of the Baths of Diocletian are still standing, but those familiar with the architectural history of Rome will be unsurprised to learn that the remains of the baths have been transformed into a series of local churches. In this case it seems that the medieval Romans believed that godliness should be next to cleanliness. In fact, one church, Santa Maria degli Angeli e dei Martiri (The Church of the Sainted Mary of the Angels and Martyrs) is part of the bath house, repurposed for prayer by none other than the great Michelangelo himself in the sixteenth century.

What makes this an essential part of any Roman tour is the adjacent Museo Nazionale Romano, which not only features many exhibits from the area and other parts of Rome besides, but it too is partly constructed from the remains of Diocletian's bathhouse. From the baths/churches/museum, head towards the car park of the nearby Termini station. There's a dusty and rather non-descript wall on one side, which is actually one of the few remaining stretches of Rome's Servian Wall. Those who like to study their ancient history while seated can do so within the local McDonald's, where another portion of the Servian Wall has been respectfully incorporated within the structure of the modern fast-food joint.

The Gardens of Maecenas and the sundry other Horti connected with that name have largely succumbed to the pressures of Rome's modern population and are built over, although some pleasant parkland remains. There's also a building once mistakenly believed to have been the Auditorium of Maecenas and sometimes still advertised as such. This appears instead to have been a *triclinium* (fancy dining room), separate from the main villa and partly sunken within the ground to save the diners from the heat of a Roman summer. Much of the statuary from the gardens has survived and can now be seen within the Capitoline Museum. This includes the famous sculpture of the Dying Gaul.

The Porta Praenestina is still there, somewhat dilapidated and now renamed the Porta Maggiore. Because it's 3 kilometres from the Colosseum, the enterprising visitor might be the only tourist around. The Tomb of the Baker has endured even longer than a hardtack loaf, so this is still around and it and the Museo delle Mura (Museum of the Walls) can both be explored at leisure. Don't expect to wander about in solitary splendour though. Even without tourists, the traffic is more than somewhat hectic.

The lower slopes of the Esquiline still contain a maze of narrow streets with tight-packed picturesque housing looming on either side. Thanks to the miracle of indoor plumbing there's no danger of chamber pots being emptied on one's head, although the pot plants perched on the balconies may present a hazard on a windy day. Anyone who can afford to live this close to the heart of Rome in the twenty-first century is certainly not an urban peasant, but, just in case, the city authorities have kept in place the huge firewall between the imperial forums and the lower slopes of the Esquiline.

The Baths of Titus made it all the way until the sixteenth century, when marble was needed for the Belvedere courtyard in the Vatican. The baths were demolished to supply the necessary material. At least after this act Pope Julius II was able to preserve some of Rome's cultural heritage by using the repurposed remains of the baths as a venue for the display of statues retrieved from other ancient sites around the city.

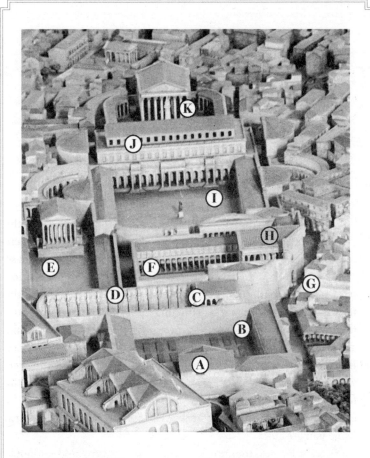

A TEMPLE OF PEACE

B FORUM OF VESPASIAN

C TEMPLE OF MINERVA

D FORUM OF NERVA

E FORUM OF CAESAR

F FORUM OF AUGUSTUS

G ARGILETUM

H TEMPLE OF MARS ULTOR

I FORUM OF TRAJAN

J LIBRARIES

K TRAJAN'S COLUMN

REGIO VIII: PART II – THE IMPERIAL FORUMS

Because One Forum Is Never Enough ...

The heart of a Roman city is the forum. At its most basic the forum is an open space in an urban environment where merchants and farmers set up their stalls on market day. Yet even in so rudimentary a site, there will be politicians explaining their position to the public, philosophers, amateur or otherwise, explaining the nature of the universe or issues of morality to anyone who will listen (the politicians probably don't). There are purse snatchers who take advantage of those distracted by acrobats and other entertainers, into which latter category the Romans put the efforts of the lawyers who argue cases before the city magistrates. In short, a visit to the forum offers the chance to see and be seen, to meet friends, to be entertained and to pick up the ingredients for your evening meal while you are at it.

Because Rome is the greatest city in the world (yes, Constantinople is trying, but it's not there yet), naturally it has the greatest forum in the world. Because Rome is also the seat of the Caesars, it is unsurprising that for propaganda purposes the emperors wanted to insert their august presence into this important aspect of everyday Roman life.

Starting with Julius Caesar himself, a succession of Caesars built their own forums as extensions to the Forum Romanum, which is the forum proper. They kept on doing this until they ran out of space. If Trajan did not exactly move mountains to build his forum, he did at least have to shift a substantial amount of hill. Thereafter, even mighty Rome had all the forums it could handle, and given that there was no more room to build any more anyway, subsequent emperors had to find other ways to impress the general public.

After yesterday's loop through the gardens of northern Rome, today we are back in the centre with a walk that starts at the top of the Forum Romanum at the Curia Julia (the Senate House) and proceeds gently eastwards through a century of forums until we cut back to Trajan's forum and the towering edifice of his column, which stands almost as tall as the depth of hillside Trajan had to remove so that he could put his monument there.

The Forum of Caesar

This is not technically an 'imperial' forum because Caesar was Dictator for Life rather than an emperor, but as his regicidally minded opponents frequently pointed out, this was a distinction without a difference. In fact, Caesar rather proved the assassins' point with this forum, for which he expropriated land from his political opponents. Until the forum stood there, this had been one of Rome's poshest residential locations. Caesar also moved the location of the Senate House and in so doing cut down the space for the *Comitium* in the forum; something else that his opponents claimed was an affront to

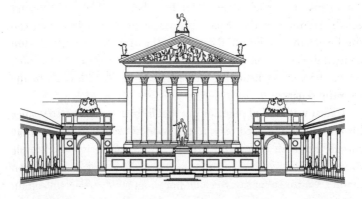

democracy. Caesar, of course, claimed that his forum was not built as a piece of self-aggrandizing propaganda but rather as a complement to the main forum that lacked certain utilities and needed more capacity in others.

Whether Rome really needed a large equestrian statue of Caesar himself is a matter of opinion, but that's what the Romans got. It has been claimed that the bronze horse upon which Caesar's image is placed was intended to represent Bucephalus, the legendary horse of Alexander the Great. This is debatable, because although Caesar saw himself as a rival to Alexander, he reckoned his own horse was itself a very distinctive animal, and that is more probably the beast represented here.

What is certainly true is that this statue was much less a public utility than were the industrial-capacity set of urinals located behind a colonnade at the south-east end of Caesar's forum. These latrines were updated by Trajan to become the largest such structure in Rome and have doubtless come as a great relief to many hard-pressed Romans over the centuries that followed.

Although actual construction of his forum began relatively late in Caesar's career, plans had been afoot since around 54 BC when Caesar started buying up property in that location. However, it took a war to forcibly persuade the last die-hards to relinquish their homes and let building begin. Not surprisingly, some senators saw the forum rising on the site of their expropriated homes as a monument commemorating their defeat, not least because Caesar thereafter usually summoned the senate to meet at the Curia Julia between this forum and the Forum Romanum. The irony that Caesar's forum abutted directly upon the Atrium Libertas (the 'House of Freedom', where the censors kept their records) was also not lost upon the resentful senate.

Caesar was fond of pointing out that he had divine ancestry, since his line could be traced back to the goddess Venus. In order to say this all the more strongly in stone, Caesar commissioned a temple to Venus Genetrix ('*genetrix*' here meaning the founder of the Julian family). Caesar never saw this building completed as by then certain members of the senate had decided that enough was enough and put an end to Caesar's career in the Curia of Pompey, in the eponymous theatre just up the road.

The forum we shall see today has been extensively remodelled since those exciting times. Caesar's adopted son and heir, the Emperor Augustus, completed the work left incomplete by Caesar's untimely death. A fire in AD 80 damaged the forum so the Emperor Domitian had the complex somewhat remodelled. This work was completed by the Emperor Trajan so that much of what you now see dates to well after Caesar's time. (The House of Freedom is gone also, removed to make way for Trajan's own, massive, forum complex.) The final touches to Caesar's forum were added by the Emperor Diocletian after yet another fire in the late third century.

The forum is used by bankers – just outside Rome is a monument to a banker mistakenly called Fortunatus (he died at age forty-two) who proudly claimed to work in this forum (Cil 6.9711). Also, the legal writer Quintilian tells us that on a busy day up to four separate legal cases could be simultaneously underway at this location.

> *He* [the orator Trachalus] *spoke so well that he was clearly audible in all four courts then in session in the Julian Forum. Though the basilica was full of noise, all four panels heard his speech and – though this does not say much for the other lawyers in the different courts – all four applauded at his conclusion.*
>
> Quintilian, *On Oratory* (10.1.119)

To get to the temple, cross the entire forum to the far wall. (This, like much else in Caesar's forum, thereafter became the standard pattern for the later imperial forums.) The temple itself is brick, although you would never know it from the gleaming marble in which it is clad. A large fountain splashes at the front with subsidiary fountains on each side. The walk to get within the temple is worth the effort (you have to go around the back, up side stairs and then around the temple colonnade to the front) because the interior is a mini art museum. On display are paintings by distinguished artists (some of which Caesar acquired while on campaign in Greece) and a statue of Caesar himself. There is also a statue of the goddess Isis, who is immediately recognizable as Caesar's royal lover, the Egyptian Queen Cleopatra, in a flimsy disguise.

The Augustan Forum

Rome's first emperor had at least two very good reasons for building his own forum even as his workmen were putting the final touches to that of Caesar's a few dozen paces away. Firstly, Augustus had seen at first-hand how popular a forum extension could be and he wanted some of that popularity for himself. Despite his usually very successful efforts to camouflage it, Augustus had basically replaced an (albeit dysfunctional) democracy with a military dictatorship, and he wanted to take people's minds off that fact. A new forum would help.

Secondly, after the assassination of his adoptive father, Julius Caesar, Augustus had vowed that if the gods allowed him retribution against Caesar's killers, he would in gratitude dedicate a temple to Mars Ultor (Mars the Avenger). After Augustus' victory over the Tyrannicides at the Battle of Philippi in 42 BC, the gods had clearly delivered on their promise, so it was now up to Augustus to keep his. Since he had to build a temple anyway, Augustus evidently decided that a new forum was the best place to put it, and he set his agents to acquiring the necessary land.

The result is a splendid forum that took over forty years from conception to completion. In fact, this forum was something of a work in progress for the next century, with various emperors tweaking or embellishing the design. One can imagine the emperor when he had some free time wandering down from the Palatine across the Forum Romanum and dropping in to see how work was going on the forum and accompanying temple. We know (from Suetonius again) that even before building was complete the forum was used to try legal cases, so between builders and stentorian lawyers this forum must have been a remarkably noisy place.

The Shape of Propaganda

One of the interesting things about following the career of Augustus is seeing how much he learned from Julius Caesar about what not to do. Caesar added to his unpopularity by pressuring or downright forcing people to yield the land he needed for his forum. Augustus, we are told (and we can be sure Augustus made certain that everyone was told), 'made his forum narrower than he had planned, because he did not want to go so far as to evict the owners of the neighbouring houses' (Suetonius, *Augustus* [56]). The resultant construction left the forum with proportions of 125 metres by 90 – less than ideal, except for propaganda purposes.

The forum is made with large blocks of peperino tufa, hidden as usual under sheets of marble. The choice of stone was because the Romans believe that this type of tufa is particularly fireproof. That huge wall against which the Temple of Mars is backed is the reverse side of that gigantic firewall that we saw in the Subura on yesterday's walk. Standing over 35 metres high, this wall both protects the forum from fire and visitors from the distressing sight of the squalid homes of the poor.

If the forum of Caesar also doubles as a gallery for great art, the forum of Augustus is something of a national portrait gallery. There are dozens and dozens of statues crowding the premises depicting almost every famous Roman of the last millennium. Furius Camillus, Cato the Elder and Tiberius Gracchus are among those who have statues here, as well as another of Augustus, slipped into the crowd as yet another Great Roman in a succession of great Romans.

Just to make sure that no one makes the mistake of confusing him with run-of-the-mill greatness, Augustus also had a separate hall built to accommodate a much larger than life statue to the Genius of Augustus. 'Genius' here has the original sense of a guiding divinity rather than signifying an egghead like Archimedes. Just to stress the point, nearby there is also a large statue of Augustus on a triumphal four-horse chariot (*quadriga*), which was dedicated to him by the senate.

The 'Forum of Mars'?

In the centuries since its construction, the Temple of Mars has become integral to the military life of the nation. When the Roman army lost three legionary eagles to a massive Germanic ambush in AD 9, Augustus spared no effort to regain the lost standards. When the lost eagles were restored after extensive pillaging expeditions across Germania, the standards were placed in the Temple of Mars the Avenger. When the senators were discussing issues of war or appointing generals, the Temple of Mars was where they usually met to do it. If those same generals were successful, then the temple was where they dedicated the spoils of victory. So essential, then, is this temple to the overall function of the Augustan forum that if you hear references to the 'Forum of Mars' this is not a landmark that you have missed on your walks, but this forum under an alternative name.

To further celebrate imperial victories over the Germans (and to conceal the fact that Rome had lost Germania as a province and was never going to get it back), triumphal arches were constructed in AD 19 by Augustus' successor, Tiberius. The later construction of the Forum of Trajan has since relieved the Forum of Augustus of many of its previous functions. Today, to a certain extent, this forum is something of a backwater in the busy life of central Rome.

Even bankers are no longer so keen on the place. At one time the *cella* of the Temple of Mars was used as a cash depository by the wealthy, although as the satirist Juvenal once snarkily remarked, the temples in the Forum Romanum are a safer bet.

> *Cash should be deposited with watchful Castor* [in his temple]
> *since Mars the Avenger lost his helmet* [to a thief] *and can't even*
> *protect his own personal effects.*

Juvenal, Satire 14 l. 260 ff

Forum of Nerva

This is the smallest of the imperial forums, but the one with the most names. It can also – and with more justice – be called the Forum of Domitian. It is also sometimes known as the Forum Palladium and many Romans call it the Forum Transitorium.

Let's go through these names. The forum was the brainchild of the Emperor Domitian who, not unreasonably, wanted his own forum, since his father and older brother had each built one of their own 45 metres away from the Forum of Augustus. So what Domitian decided to do was to build his own forum between the other two. If Augustus complained that his forum was a touch too narrow for perfect form, Domitian's forum was an out-and-out monster, being almost as long as the forum of Augustus (114 metres) but from necessity only 45 metres wide. Furthermore, this forum had also to accommodate an important and ancient Roman thoroughfare, the *Argiletum* (clay road), which connects the Subura and upper Esquiline Hill with the Forum Romanum, which it enters alongside the Basilica Aemilia. On the Esquiline side, you might like to check if the shop where the poet Martial sold his books is still in existence. He writes in his *Epigrams*:

> *To be sure of obtaining* [a copy]. *Seek Secundus, the freedman of*
> *the learned Lucensis, behind the Temple of Peace and the Forum*
> *of Pallas ... You prefer, little book, to dwell in the shops in the*
> *Argiletum ...*

Martial, Epigrams (12. 2&3 passim)

Because Domitian could not actually block off so important a road, he had to accommodate it within his forum design. Hence the next

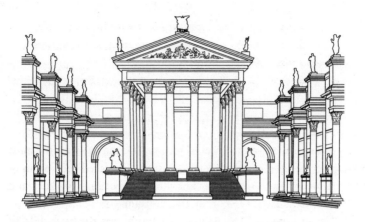

name for this forum, the Forum Transitorium: many Romans use
Domitian's creation as a sort of glorified boulevard to transit from
the Esquiline to the Forum Romanum or to get between the various
imperial forums, since Domitian's connects with three of the other
four. Incidentally, another major thoroughfare runs through, or
rather under, this forum. That's the Cloaca Maxima, which carries
the waste of the Subura to the Tiber River.

This leads us, by way of a misogynistic quote attributed to the
Church father Tertullian, to another name for this forum. In a
particular rant, Tertullian (c. AD 150–220) is said to have referred to
'woman' – in general or particular – as a 'temple built over a sewer'.
While this is often construed as a general-purpose insult, it may in
fact refer to a particular temple of a particular female deity.

That deity is the Roman goddess Minerva and the temple in
question is that in Domitian's forum. Domitian was a henotheist
– that is, someone who believes in a complete pantheon of gods
but prefers to worship one in particular. For Domitian that deity
was Minerva, and it was naturally her temple that he built at the
north end of his forum, right over the sewer of the Cloaca Maxima.
Minerva was the Roman equivalent of the Greek goddess Pallas
Athena, which is why this forum is sometimes called the Forum of
Pallas or the Palladium.

Domitian never saw the completion of his forum. It seems that he was wrong to trust his safety to the aegis of Minerva, since he was assassinated in AD 96. His forum was completed by his successor the Emperor Nerva. Once the building was completed, Nerva named the forum – which had largely been built by Domitian – after himself. This was not so much copyright theft as brand protection, because by the time of his death Domitian was monumentally unpopular. Naming a major new landmark in Rome in his much-despised memory would not have gone down well. So the Forum of Nerva this forum became, and the Forum of Nerva it has (mostly) remained thereafter.

The extreme narrowness of this forum made it impossible for Domitian's architect (who was probably Domitian's favourite in this field, one Rabirius) to construct a proper portico running alongside the walls. Instead, cunning optics have been deployed to make a fake portico of almost fifty marble columns. This portico almost looks as if you could walk under it until you try and find that the thing is only half a pace wide. This fake does expand into a genuine portico (the Arch of Nerva) just where the forum opens up to the Subura.

Perhaps the best feature of this forum is the frieze that runs along the upper levels depicting various myths connected with Athena/ Minerva. However, the female figure with helmet and shield – one of several females similarly depicted along the walls of the forum – is not Minerva, even though she is often depicted in similar attire. This character is Pirusta, who personifies a region in the Balkans, rather as Britannia depicts that distant island to the north-west of the empire. By displaying statues personifying regions of the empire, Domitian seems to have been attempting to encompass his whole realm within this one space. To these statues a later emperor, Severus Alexander, had added equestrian statues of Rome's greatest emperors. Don't bother looking for Domitian among them though. Severus Alexander didn't want to remind people about an assassinated emperor (not that it helped – he too was assassinated in AD 235).

The eastern part of the forum takes us to the next destination of our walk – the Forum of Peace, also known as the Forum of Vespasian.

The Forum of Vespasian

This forum pre-dates that of Domitian to the west and is dominated by the Temple of Peace, which stands squarely in the middle. The 'peace' referred to here is neatly described in an aphorism of the historian Tacitus who remarked that the Romans were in the habit of subduing rebellious peoples by 'creating a devastation and calling it peace'. It has to be admitted that Judea was remarkably peaceful after Vespasian and his son Titus had finished off the Jewish rebellion of AD 66–73. Demolished buildings and streets lined with corpses don't make a lot of noise.

A Bolt from the Blue

Perhaps it is that the destruction of a temple is particularly shocking, but temples in Rome do seem to have rather a tough time. As well as Jupiter using his own temple for target practice with his thunderbolts, it seems he had it in for Vespasian's temple also.

Although no dark clouds gathered to warn of a thunderstorm (though an earth tremor presaged the event), a lightning bolt at night or a fire caused by the earth tremor almost totally destroyed the Temple of Peace, the largest and most beautiful building in Rome.

It was the richest of all the temples, and, because it was a safe place, it was filled with votive offerings of gold and silver and everyone deposited their treasures within. Therefore in just one night this one fire made paupers of many rich men. All Rome mourned the public loss, and many individuals mourned their private one.

Herodian, *Roman History* (1.14.2&3)

Vespasian vowed to build his temple once the Jewish war was complete, and the work was done by Jewish prisoners using money looted from Judea. To some degree the temple itself is a museum of that war because many of the exhibits displayed inside are trophies taken by the victorious legions. These include a large golden menorah allegedly taken from the sacred temple in Jerusalem.

The forum faces towards the Velian ridge and that other great memorial to the Flavian family, the great amphitheatre in the Colosseum area. Many visitors to the temple come to view the memorabilia of the Jewish war but stay for the statuary. This is because at the same time as he was building his forum, Vespasian was also demolishing the Golden House of Nero, his ill-famed predecessor. For Nero only the best would do, so his house and very extensive gardens were adorned with statues by the greatest artists in Greece and Rome. The names of Myron, Polykleitos and Phidias are spoken with awe by later sculptors, and their works and those of only somewhat lesser artists were beautifully showcased by Nero.

When Nero's masterwork of a residence was demolished and its remains converted to public use, the statues had to go somewhere and the forum of Vespasian was where a lot of them ended up. Vespasian's architects did their best, but the pink walls of Aswan marble that enclose the forum don't show these great sculptures in their best light, with each sculpture really needing a bit more space to be appreciated individually.

The 'forum' part of the name is a bit of a misnomer because little forum-style business is done at this location. It is really a temple-plus-museum. Most of the temple you see today actually dates to the early third century after the original was practically destroyed by a disastrous fire.

Fortunately the temple was rebuilt, probably by the Emperor Septimius Severus (who also had good reason for wanting to be associated with Peace after a devastating civil war), and many later writers still describe this temple as one of the most beautiful in a city filled with beautiful buildings.

The Forum of Trajan

Vespasian had a forum, Nerva had – or rather had inherited – a forum, so Nerva's successor Trajan (AD 98–117) naturally wanted a forum of his own, too. Trajan's problem was that central Rome was running out of space for forum development, especially as he was a man who did not think small. Just as Trajan was determined to be Rome's greatest emperor (he added the provinces of Dacia and Mesopotamia to expand the Roman empire to its greatest extent), he determined that his forum would outshine the others in size and grandeur – if only he could find somewhere to put the thing.

Trajan consulted with his pet architect, Apollodorus of Damascus. (This is that same Apollodorus who was later executed for his harsh critique of Hadrian's forays into architecture.) Apollodorus pointed out that the space between the Capitoline and the Quirinal hills was free. That is, apart from a ridge of rock that connected the two hills. Fortunately for Trajan he had the resources of an empire at his disposal and plenty of slave labourers captured during his Dacian war. These labourers toiled to extract hundreds of tons of rock and hundreds of thousands of cubic metres of soil until they had created a piazza some 55,000 square metres in size. That is, about ten times the size of Nerva's forum. The major part of this excavation was not the ridge, which was relatively puny, but the Quirinal Hill itself: Trajan's builders took a large bite out of it to get the size of forum their imperial master wanted.

Enter this wonder of Roman architecture from the south, if looping back from the Temple of Peace via the Forum Romanum, or through an archway and portico if coming from the Forum of Augustus. The southern entrance is preferable because it is designed to impress, and as a tourist you may as well enjoy the full effect. The forum is partly screened from view by a large triumphal archway commemorating Trajan's Dacian war. This arch would by itself be rated as one of Rome's premier monuments if it stood alone elsewhere. It is a three-arch structure, with decorative statuary in the niches, and topped by a larger-than-life statue of Trajan in a six-horse chariot. Not unexpectedly, this arch takes up most of the view until you get through it and are suddenly in a vast, three-sided enclosure with towering walls and a floor all encased in light-reflecting marble.

Originally this forum broke with tradition by not having a temple as its centrepiece, but Trajan's conservatively minded successors made good the lack by adding to the forum a small but elegant temple dedicated to the memory of the deified Trajan himself.

Making an Impression

Here's how Trajan's forum affected one distinguished visitor, the Emperor Constantius, when he entered Rome for the first time:

Then, as he surveyed the sections of the city ... he thought that whatever next met his gaze towered above all the rest ... the Forum of Peace, the Theatre of Pompey, the Odeum, the Circus Maximus and, amongst these, the other adornments of the Eternal City.

But when he came to the Forum of Trajan, a construction unique under the heavens, as we believe, and admirable even in the unanimous opinion of the gods, he stood rooted by amazement ... abandoning all hope of attempting anything like it, he said that he would and could copy Trajan's steed alone, which stands in the centre of the vestibule, carrying the emperor himself.

Ammianus Marcellinus, *History* (16.10.14)
(Text adapted from the J.C. Rolfe translation of 1935)

You will have noticed that the walls of the forum are not sheer marble cliffs – they are in fact multi-storey colonnades built into the side of the hill. The most significant of these is the Market of Trajan, which was built as an integral part of the forum. Here you will find a variety of high-class shops selling everything from rare spices to silks and exotic jewellery. Also, on a different level are a series of offices where imperial officials administer civic matters such as distribution of the corn dole to the citizens.

Enter through the east side for the basilica, tastefully decorated in white and yellow marble, with around 100 columns in the same colour. The roof of this building is mentioned in an aside by the second-century travel writer Pausanias who describes Trajan's Forum as 'worth seeing not only for its general beauty but especially for its roof made of bronze' (Pausanias [5.12.6]).

On then to the north part of this forum and the Ulpian library, which is generally considered as second only to the library of Alexandria as a repository of knowledge. There are, for example, tens of thousands of books and scrolls dealing only with centuries of civic matters within the city. The library is divided, as is traditional, into Greek and Roman sections. Both sections have a view from the windows of one of the most remarkable tombs in Rome, that of Trajan himself.

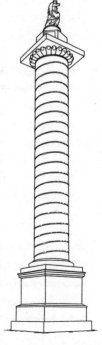

One does not think of Trajan's Column as a tomb, but that is what it is – the ashes of the emperor and his wife are interred in the base. This, as it happens, is an advantage of the forum's location – part of it lies outside the sacred *pomerium* of Rome, within which burials are forbidden. Trajan's column is very adjacent to, but outside, the *pomerium*. The column towers to the height of the excavations into the hillside – just over 100 feet. This is fortunate, as you can ascend the levels of the library and market and, as you go, follow the spiralling picture story that winds up the column.

You can also go winding up the column from the inside on the narrow winding stair that leads to the small platform at the top. Small windows give a view of the forum as you move up the stairwell, and at the top you can verify for yourself the claim on the inscription at the bottom.

[From] *the Senate and people of Rome to the Emperor Caesar ...*
Traianus Augustus Germanicus Dacicus ... to demonstrate what
great height of the hill was removed for such a great work.

The outside of the column is the story of Trajan's most famous
campaign, showing in pictures how his legions crossed the Danube,
besieged cities and fought battles all the way up to the death of
the Dacian leader Decebalus and the capture of his capital city. If,
after viewing this column and the setting in which it is placed, you
remain unawed by the grandeur, power and majesty of Rome, even
tomorrow's walk through the Palatine won't cut it. Trajan's forum is
as good as it gets.

From here, exit the imperial forums and head back to the nearby
baths of Constantine to finish today's walk.

THE TWENTY-FIRST CENTURY WALK

The first thing today's tourist notes about the modern site of the
imperial forums is that someone has constructed a four-lane highway
that runs straight through it. That someone was Mussolini who,
although he ended his career dangling from a lamp post for other
reasons, deserved to be hanged for this atrocity alone.

Fortunately, the modern curators of Rome's heritage are more
responsible, and the pleas and imprecations of archaeologists and
conservationists have caused them to limit traffic on the road. This
in turn has limited – but not completely stopped – the consequent
damage from pollution and vibration that this highway causes to
the ancient structures that it runs alongside and, occasionally, over.
Therefore, the first thing that a visitor to the forums must work out
is how to get across from the Esquiline without becoming roadkill
along the way (Roman drivers take no prisoners). Fortunately, the
Via Argiletum is still in business after adding a couple of thousand
years to its already ancient resume.

Approaching the forum along this street gives you a view of the
last classical addition to the Roman Forum, the Column of Phocas,

which was added in the seventh century. You'll also see in the stone of the Via Argiletum ruts worn by medieval carts that carried stone taken from the forum for other purposes. As a result of those depredations and general dilapidation by time, the most conspicuous remnant of Caesar's forum, apart from the almost intact Senate House of the Curia Julia, are three lonely columns of the Temple of Venus Genetrix. (The Curia survived by becoming the Church of St Adrian in the seventh century.) The forum of Augustus is now best approached through the little side street of the Via Alessandrina, which mostly consists of a wide set of steps to a temple that – apart from a few columns - isn't there anymore, and the impressive firewall behind, which very definitely is. Of Vespasian's Temple of Peace, there is little to see: mostly a flat area with some random stones. Certainly there is nothing that a Roman of the classical era would have recognized.

As with the other imperial forums, much of what remained on the site has been taken away, but fortunately not very far. The fragments are now in the Museum of the Imperial Fora (near where Trajan's market still stands), which does an excellent job of preserving the remains of the forums and of showing how they might have looked in their heyday.

In the forum of Nerva, many of the columns in the fake portico have survived, as well as part of the Minerva frieze that decorated the top section. The surviving piece tells the story of Arachne, a skilled weaver who had the audacity to challenge Athena at weaving and was turned into the first spider for her pains. As to the temple of Minerva, this still serves a holy function, although the temple itself was dismantled at the start of the seventeenth century. But some of the stonework is now built into St Peter's on the Vatican.

The recycling into the Vatican of the imperial forums and other sites continued under Pope Urban VIII (1623–44). This led to a famous protest in Latin against the aristocratic Barberini clan to which Urban belonged. Even today you may hear a Roman tour guide mutter, '*Quod non fecerunt barbari, fecerunt Barberini*' ('What the barbarians did not do was done by the Barberine').

Trajan's forum has fared somewhat better than its imperial companions. The column is still there, towering over the remains of Trajan's forum, although the statue of Trajan that once topped off the structure was replaced by St Peter in 1588. The Greek and Latin libraries from which the column could once be viewed are now gone, so binoculars are now needed to view the thousands of figures portrayed on the bas-relief (which would be 200 metres long if unwound from the column). Alternatively, one can travel to the Museo della Civiltà Romana in Rome's Esposizione Universale Roma district. Here, casts of the entire sculpture are at eye level for easy viewing. However, repairs to this museum have taken almost as long as did the construction of Trajan's forum in the first place, so check how work is doing before making the trip.

Trajan's market (sometimes called 'the world's first shopping mall') is still open to customers – that is, to tourists paying around €15 for a ticket, a price that includes entry to the museum of the Imperial Fora. In previous centuries the market has served as the residence of an aristocratic Roman family, as a fortress that was later converted to a convent for noble ladies and then to a barracks. Now restored to as close as possible to its original format, this market and forum is, as it was 1,500 years ago, the most impressive of the imperial forums.

REGIONES IX & XI:
THE CIRCUS FLAMINIUS TO
THE CATTLE MARKET

The Theatre District and More

Today's walk begins at the very edge of Regio IX, with the sun rising over Rome's most northerly racetrack, the Circus Flaminius. Although a popular and well-attended venue, it is totally lacking the awesome size and reputation of the final stop on tomorrow's walk: the Circus Maximus, Rome's premier venue for chariot racing.

We start on the road of the Porticus Maximus at the edge of the Campus Martius, Rome's military training field, voting area and general playground. Before us is Rome's 'theatre district', including two of the most imposing theatres ever built, where the works of Seneca, Sophocles and Euripides entertain the highbrows and bawdy pantomimes amuse the *grex vulgaris* (the common herd).

Odeon of Domitian

On the left, the brown waters of the Tiber can be glimpsed between towering apartment buildings and to the right is the Odeon of Domitian. This first of the theatrical venues is well liked by theatrical cognoscenti for its relatively cosy atmosphere. Even a sold-out performance can pack in only 4,000 spectators, while the theatres down the road hold at least five times more.

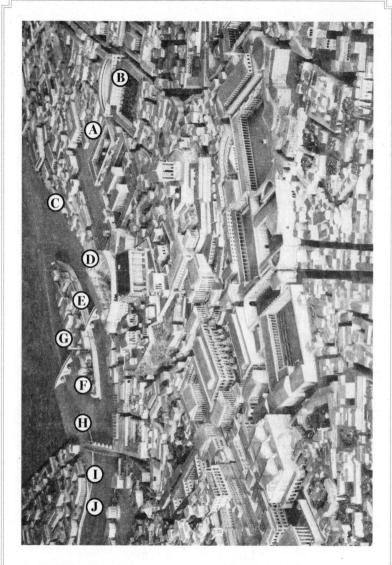

A THEATRE OF POMPEY
B POMPEY'S PORTICO
C THE NAVALIA
D THEATRE OF MARCELLUS
E PONS FABRICUS
F TEMPLE OF AESCULAPIUS
G THE OBELISK
H PONS AEMILIUS
I TEMPLE OF PORTUNUS
J TEMPLE OF HERCULES

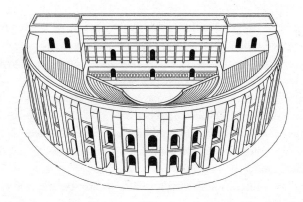

An odeon is a special type of theatre dedicated to Apollo, god of the musical arts. The name comes from the Greek, as does an awful lot of Roman culture. Odeon means 'singing place' and because of this emphasis on music, odeons are roofed to provide a better auditory experience (the average theatre is open-air).

This odeon was built by the Emperor Domitian, whose Flavian dynasty was despised by the snobbish Roman senate as plebeian upstarts who had seized the purple after the death of the despicable (but very highly bred) Nero. If the odeon was Domitian's attempt to ingratiate himself with the cultured elite, he failed; he was assassinated in AD 96 to general aristocratic applause.

Soon after his death, the odeon was damaged by fire, possibly as a result of vengeful vandalism or perhaps in one of those random blazes which plague the city. However, the Emperor Trajan's top architect, Apollodorus, effected restorations, and today the historian Ammianus Marcellinus ranks Domitian's Odeon as Rome's premier theatrical venue.

Theatre of Pompey

The buildings alongside the Tiber have an industrial appearance because centuries ago this was the *Navalia,* the shipyard where Rome's warships were built before sailing down the Tiber to battle with the fleets of Carthage.

Ahead is the porticus for which this street is named. This porticus is a covered walkway stretching over 100 yards alongside the massive bulk of the Theatre of Pompey and itself capable of sheltering thousands of people from the elements.

The Theatre of Pompey is open to the sky because theoretically it is not a theatre at all. Like all generals of the late Roman Republic, Pompey was also a politician, and his theatre was designed to convert some of the fortune he had looted from his eastern conquests into political capital with Roman voters.

At the time, Rome lacked a decent theatre because the censors and aediles (the latter being responsible for the city's buildings) frowned upon such establishments. They felt Roman citizens should watch a play standing up, as befitted a nation of warriors, rather than lounging about on seats like decadent wimps. Consequently, early Roman plays were rather ad hoc affairs staged in the forum before a fickle audience could rush off if someone nearby was showing off acrobats or gladiators. In fact, the playwright Terence gets quite bitter about this in the prologue to one of his plays:

> I again present you the 'Hecyra', which I have never been allowed to act before you in silence ... The first time, when I began this play, the boasts of boxers, excitement about a coming rope-dancer, all on top of the throng of followers, the racket, the clamour of the women, caused me to retire early from your presence.

Terence, Hecyra (Prologue 1)

Knowing that a theatre would violate the *mos maiorum* (roughly translatable as 'the ancestral tradition'), which the Romans deeply respect, Pompey instead built a temple to Venus, the goddess of love. This temple was a relatively small edifice with a disproportionately massive set of steps leading to the front door. These steps were ideal for anyone who wanted to bring a cushion and sit on them while watching a play on the stage below. The acoustics of the side walls reflected the words of the actors to the audience because they were

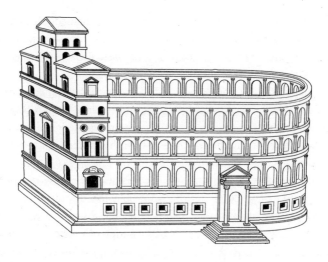

designed to do exactly that, but Pompey wasn't upfront about their real purpose.

Plutarch records that the temple opened with great ceremony, the large crowds entertained by gymnastic displays, literary events, wild beast hunts and a spectacular fight between two elephants. As the historian Velleius Paterculus remarked, had Pompey perished immediately afterwards, he would have been forever considered one of Rome's greatest sons.

In fact, Pompey died after being defeated in a civil war by Julius Caesar. Yet, he got a sort of posthumous revenge. Pompey's theatre was an entire entertainment complex with a gymnasium, library and a meeting place for city officials, which included the senate. On the Ides of March 44 BC, Julius Caesar was assassinated here at the foot of a statue of Pompey. According to Suetonius, Caesar's eventual successor, the Emperor Augustus, later placed this statue over the so-called 'Royal Door' to the theatre proper. Here you can stand by that statue and imagine the scene when Nero entertained the king of Armenia, as described by the Roman senator and historian Cassius Dio in his *History*:

> *Not merely the stage but the entire theatre was gilded, so people afterwards referred to that as the 'Golden Day'. Even the props and everything brought in were of gold. The velae* [literally 'sails' of cloth] *stretched overhead to keep out the sun were purple. Embroidered into the central shade was a figure of Nero driving a chariot surrounded by golden stars. Afterwards there was a splendid banquet.*

According to the Elder Pliny, the theatre can accommodate some 40,000 people who know each other really well – but with proper social distancing, half that number is more reasonable. Much of the theatre, such as the columns ascending in the Doric, Ionic and Corinthian styles, level by level, remains as built by Pompey. However, time and at least two major fires have led to extensive restorations, with each restoration making the theatre more grand.

The next theatre in the district is that of Caesar's chum, the Spanish senator Balbus, and is notable only for the columns of rare and expensive onyx that caused quite a stir when they were first erected.

The Creation of the Amphitheatre

After Pompey's theatre set the precedent, there was a rash of theatre building in Rome. One construction worth mentioning was a temporary affair from which the audience watched a play from not one but two sets of seats curved around the stage. Then, without the audience leaving their seats, they were treated to a gladiator display in an arena created by the two curved sets of seats being wheeled together to form a closed oval. The enclosure formed by both (*amphi*) sets of seats gives us the word 'amphitheatre'.

Theatre of Marcellus

Rome's first emperor, Augustus Caesar, noted the political impact of Pompey's theatre upon the Roman people. Indeed, in his *Res Gestae*, his list of personal achievements, he stresses that he himself contributed to the embellishment of that theatre.

Augustus' first choice of heir was his nephew Marcellus, who inconveniently died of illness. Some six years after Marcellus' death, Augustus decided to erect a theatre in his nephew's memory. It helped that some of the preliminary work had been done by Julius Caesar (who also knew a thing or two about ingratiating himself with the crowd). Caesar had purchased the land and removed a small but inconvenient temple before being assassinated just up the road.

Although construction only started in 17 BC, the theatre was complete enough to stage events of the Secular Games just a few years later.

Starting on the Wrong Foot

The opening of the Theatre of Marcellus was inauspicious. When Augustus sat on his dedicated chair, it collapsed and sent him sprawling. At a later event, the audience panicked that the walls were leaning inwards (an optical illusion) and were about to crush them. Although unjustified in this case, there were enough jerry-built structures in Rome at the time for this to be a reasonable suspicion. Augustus failed to pacify the crowd until he left his seat and watched the proceedings from the most 'dangerous' part of the structure.

Like most major buildings in Rome, the Theatre of Marcellus is made of travertine stone, limestone quarried from near Tibur (modern Tivoli). Travertine is derived from the Latin for 'from

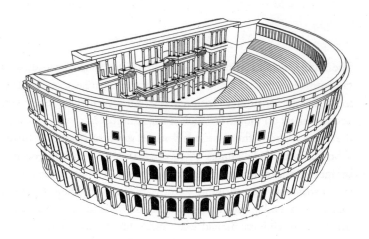

Tibur'. Limestone – and local limestone at that – is not glamorous enough for a prestigious Roman building, so there's little of it on display. Yet behind the veneer of marble and stucco are tons of solid Roman rock. There's also fired brick in the facade, because at the time of the theatre's construction this was a novelty imported from the Greek world. Overall, the theatre is built with a solidity that will hold it steady through the millennia.

Despised – and Adored

Theatre is enjoyed by all classes in Rome, although actors have the same dubious reputation as gladiators and charioteers. Everyone agrees they are morally suspect and social outcasts, yet sponsors and spectators pay top members of these professions ludicrous sums to appear before their hordes of adoring fans. When the Emperor Vespasian staged a series of theatrical productions at the Theatre of Marcellus, his biographer recorded that tens of thousands of sesterces were paid to the top actors. By way of comparison, a contemporary Roman legionary was paid around 1,000 sesterces a month.

Tiber Island

The Theatre of Marcellus is built along an axis running north-west to south-east, directly along an imaginary line between the golden-roofed temple of Jupiter Optimus Maximus on the Capitoline Hill and the island on the River Tiber, usually and unimaginatively called the Tiber Island, although the full name is not any better - 'Insula Tiberina Inter Duos Pontes' (the island on the Tiber between two bridges). At least Rome's engineers have shown more imagination in construction than in nomenclature, because the island has been shaped to resemble a gigantic ship, eternally sailing in place down the river. To reinforce the illusion, there is an obelisk where the ship would have had a mast if it was indeed going somewhere.

The island is approached by the Fabrician Bridge. This bridge is also a destination in itself. Stand at one end and you stand where the Roman soldier and nobleman Horatius Cocles, in days of old, held the bridge against an Etruscan army determined to overthrow Rome's new Republic. The Romans had just evicted King Tarquin and, perhaps fearing that his own citizens might follow this bad example, King Lars Porsenna of Etruria staged a surprise march on Rome. The only way across the Tiber was over the Fabrician Bridge, which the Romans hastened to demolish. To keep the enemy off the bridge, three heroic Romans led by Horatius held off the entire enemy army. (The incident was immortalized by the Victorian poet Macaulay in his *Lays of Ancient Rome*.)

At the other end of the bridge, you'll be near where the famed orator and politician Cicero stood to view the reconstruction of the bridge in 62 BC, in the year of his consulship. The bridge was reconstructed because the older version was made of wood – which is how the Romans were able to hew down the bridge behind Horatius, who finished his epic stand by swimming across the Tiber to safety. In later centuries one Lucius Fabricius, the curator of the roads in Rome, had the bridge rebuilt in its present form, which included the engineering innovation of building the arches in spans wider than the semi-circular arch previously used in stone bridges. The 62-metre bridge is made of trusty travertine stone, reinforced in places by tufa – another traditional Roman building material. To make his mark with posterity, Fabricius had his name and rank carved on each of the bridge's four arches. The bridge has taken a few blows over the years, starting with severe damage from floods a generation after its construction. Father Tiber resents being denied the ages-old flood plain that has become the Roman Forum, so the banks alongside the Tiber have been built up to contain the river. That walkway running alongside and under the bridge is not designed for a pleasant evening stroll (although most times it works well for this), but to give the river extra room for expansion as the seasonal flood comes roaring through.

For most of the history of the Roman Republic, the Tiber Island was only connected to the eastern bank and the city of Rome proper, but at about the same time as the bridge was reconstructed, a sister bridge was added to the western side of the island, so now the Pons Cestius completes the crossing of the Tiber.

According to *From the Founding of the City* by the historian Livy (who may have underestimated the local sense of humour), the island was created after Rome's last king, the tyrannical Tarquinius Superbus, had been overthrown:

> *The traditional land of the Tarquin family between the City and the Tiber was consecrated to Mars ... because the land was now dedicated to the god, the crop could not be used for human*

> *consumption. So a large gang of workmen was set to the task of mowing the crop to the ground … and carrying it away in basketloads, which were dumped in the Tiber.*
>
> *As usual in midsummer the river was down to a weak flow, insufficient to carry the grain away downstream. Instead the huge mound settled into the mud where it accumulated a mass of the usual debris that a river carries downstream. These gradually grew to the point where an actual island was formed … high above water level and made it strong enough to bear the weight of temples and porticos.*

Those of a less romantic disposition might note that Tiber Island is in fact a 300-metre-long ridge of hard rock that became an island when the river cut into the alluvial soil of the valley between the Seven Hills. Rome is at the head of navigation, at the point where it becomes impossible for seagoing ships to proceed further upriver (because there's a large island in the way). For the same reason, this was the first point where the Tiber became bridgeable, making this location a vital link between the ancient salt pans at Ostia and the hills of the interior – and one reason why Rome was founded where it was.

The Romans have for centuries used the island as a sort of isolation ward for cases of infectious disease within the city. Consequently, there is now a temple to the god Aesculapius where the sick receive at least some basic medical attention. The Emperor Claudius long ago decreed that owners who dumped sick slaves at the temple would lose possession of them if the sufferers recovered. Indeed, as most priests of Aesculapius treat their patients with hygiene, fresh air and a healthy diet, quite a remarkable number do recover.

Naturally, the Romans could not resist embellishing the foundation of the hospital/temple with a juicy legend and the tale goes back to 300 BC. At that time, Rome was suffering from a plague so devastating that the senate decreed that the Sibylline Books should be consulted. These books dated back to Rome's legendary past and were allegedly sold to King Tarquin Superbus by a mysterious Sybil ('Sybil' being a generic term for a female seer or prophet). The books have acted as Rome's emergency disaster manual ever since. In this case, according to the books, ambassadors were to proceed to the Greek city of Epidaurus and 'bring back Aesculapius', the god of healing. The ambassadors were looking for a representation of the god – ideally a sacred statue. What they got was a snake that took up residence on the Roman ship and showed no intention of leaving. Snakes in Graeco-Roman culture are keepers of arcane knowledge, which is why a snake is entwined about Aesculapius' staff. So, when the snake on the ambassadors' ship was determined to have come from the temple of the healing god, the Romans accepted his clear instructions and brought the snake to Rome. On the way up the Tiber, the snake slipped overboard and swam to Tiber Island, where it ensconced itself in a palm tree. The Romans took the hint and erected their temple to Aesculapius on the spot. After which the plague ended.

Tiber Island is outside the *pomerium*. This means that the temple there can be used for meetings of the senate that cannot happen within the city. The senate can meet on any sacred ground (such as the temple dedicated for that purpose at the Theatre of Pompey), but some people to whom the senators want to talk cannot enter the city – for example, kings or Roman generals under arms. (The Romans felt that allowing a serving general and his men into the city constituted too much of a temptation to any would-be dictator planning a coup.)

The Temple of Aesculapius was upgraded when the Fabrician Bridge was converted into a stone bridge and the island will care for the sick through the coming millennia. Another small temple on the island is that to Tiberinus, the divine embodiment of the River Tiber.

The Romans show little respect for the river. Father Tiber (as the Romans like to call the river) is the city's dustman, carrying household refuse, dead dogs and the occasional corpse out to the sea. The Cloaca Maxima – Rome's great drainage sewer – discharges directly into the Tiber, making the nutrient-rich water at this point a primary breeding ground for lampreys. These fish are a delicacy at Roman tables and a good example of direct recycling.

How the Tiber Got its Name

The Tiber is the third longest river in Italy, a watercourse that takes its name from King Tiberinus Silvius of the now-vanished city of Alba Longa. Tiberinus was the ninth king of that city, which is famous in Roman myth as the place where the city's founders, Romulus and Remus, were born. King Tiberinus ruled some 200 years before his famous descendants went on to found Rome. He drowned while crossing the river, which back then was called the Albula. Soon it became clear that the king was drowned but not dead. He had instead become a river deity, the spiritual manifestation of the river that had taken him. Therefore, the river has been called the Tiber ever since.

The guild of those who go fishing and diving for salvage in the Tiber annually celebrate the Ludi Piscatorii (Fishermen's Games) in June, at around the same time that the Shrine of the Vestal Virgins in the Forum gets its annual spring cleaning, the debris from which is solemnly and ceremonially deposited into the river. A month later is the ceremony of the Tiberinalia when the river and its patron deity are themselves honoured.

Before the river gets too polluted, energetic Romans swim in the waters upstream where the riverbank is lined by the villas of the wealthy, with gardens stretching down to the banks. Here Julius Caesar honed his aquatic skills by swimming across the Tiber as a boy.

Some 200 yards downstream from Tiber Island, the river takes a sharp bend back to the south. (The Tiber usually runs north to south, but curves briefly to run east to west past the Tiber Island.) Here we recross to the east bank while admiring the durability of the stonework of the Pons Aemilius, Rome's oldest stone bridge. This bridge was constructed during the second century, at around the time that the Via Aurelia was completed. The Via Aurelia runs right through Rome, and the increased traffic on the creaky wooden bridge demanded a sturdier replacement. Scipio Aemilianus, the Roman general and politician mostly famous for the final destruction of Punic Carthage in 146 BC, was among those who financed the bridge's distinctive arches.

The Forum Boarium

Once across the river, you will be standing on the edge of Rome's main livestock market, the Forum Boarium. This bustling (and aromatic, even by Roman standards) site was the location of the original harbour of Rome, the Portus Tiberinus. Barges laden with cattle, sheep and other assorted animals destined for the Roman dinner table arrive every day. There is a constant bustle as traders and butchers haggle over prices, although everyone treads carefully around enclosures where a bull has a twist of hay tied around one horn – the warning sign of a dangerous animal.

The forum is older than Rome itself: Hercules, returning from one of his labours with a herd of stolen cattle, was unsuccessfully ambushed here by the robber Cacus.

Another early visitor to the forum was Aeneas, the ancestor of Romulus and Remus, sent by the poet Virgil to take a look at the site of the future city. At the Forum Boarium, Aeneas met Evander, the local king, and was taken around the seven hills. The pair departed from the forum along the pathway that is now the Vicus Iugarius road, passing by the shrine to the nymph Carmenta. This Carmenta was the mother of Evander and the grandmother of that Pallas after whom the Palatine Hill was named. She was famous for her prophetic ability, and even now has a temple beside the gate that later became the Porta Carmentalis of Rome.

Next in this forum we come to the Temple to Portunus, the god of harbours, locks (the type barges go through) and granaries, which was one of several upgrades in the first century BC as it converted a somewhat squelchy cattle market to something more approaching the dignity of an imperial city.

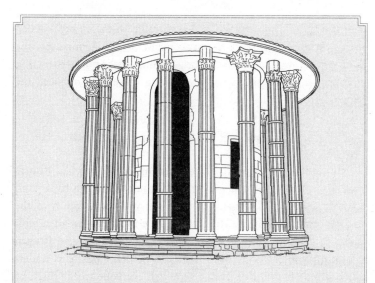

A Temple Older than Rome

The site of the messy demise of Cacus is marked by a temple called the Temple of Hercules Victor. The present temple was rebuilt in stone in the second century BC, although the circular design shows that the original was much, much older. Later Roman temples are basically a box with a columned portico in front – albeit a very beautiful box with all sorts of architectural subtleties and complex mathematical proportions. The temple to Hercules has a fragile charm so unlike the oafish hero that later ages will assume instead that it was a shrine to Vesta. The circular shape was originally formed by upright logs and still has a conical roof, now of tiles, but once woven out of branches.

Also in the somewhat gentrified Forum Boarium is a statue by the Greek sculptor Myron. In contrast to his other statues, such as the famous *discobolus* (the Discus Thrower), the statue in the Forum Boarium has an appropriately bovine theme. (The other statues and copies of statues by Myron are dotted around Rome and the thoughtful tourist can easily put in a day's wandering to spot them all.)

The Porta Trigemina, the three-arched gateway through the Servian Wall, admits the constant stream of road traffic from the port at Ostia. This location hosts a swarm of beggars taking advantage of the generosity of travellers relieved to have finally arrived in Rome. This is also the point at which the Cloaca Maxima discharges the contents of thousands of Roman bowels into the Tiber, adding its own distinctive aroma to the already pungent atmosphere of the cattle market.

Uphill, in the cleaner air of the Aventine Hill, enjoy a view of tomorrow's premier attraction: the Circus Maximus. Pass by two other attractions awaiting you, the temples of Flora and Mercury, as your destination is the Baths of Sura where you can soak away the stresses of the day in the waters of this small but well-appointed establishment.

THE TWENTY-FIRST CENTURY WALK

The first point mentioned on this walk, the Circus Flaminius, has altogether vanished so comprehensively now that no one is sure exactly where it was. The remains of an arcade later built into medieval shops were once assumed to be part of the circus, but are now recognized as part of the Theatre of Balbus.

The Odeon of Domitian has fared somewhat better, in that its location is known. The solid Roman foundations now support the Palazzo Massimo alle Colonne and it is believed that some of the stonework of this building is recycled odeon. To get to the Theatre of Pompey from here it is a short walk down the Via dei Baullari, although apart from a few nondescript ruins there is not a lot left here either.

At the Theatre of Marcellus things get interesting, because the theatre is still there and again hosting theatrical performances after 2,000 years. When Rome turned Christian in the third and fourth centuries, theatre fell out of favour, but the demand for travertine stone did not. Consequently, some of the theatre is currently spread around in local houses and churches. The theatre was saved from total destruction by the semi-anarchic conditions prevailing in early medieval Rome. The solid structure and limited number of entrances made the theatre a relatively secure location that was converted into a family fortress.

Where the ancient audiences sat is now subterranean because the medieval Romans were not very good at taking away their trash and street levels have risen by one storey. Because of all the changes in use, the theatre looks very different from the building of 2,000 years ago. Anyone wanting to see something close to the original Theatre of Marcellus should proceed to Oxford in the United Kingdom. There, the University of Oxford's Sheldonian Theatre (completed in 1669) was consciously modelled by Sir Christopher Wren upon the original Roman design.

The Fabrician Bridge is still standing thousands of years later and is now called the Ponte dei Quattro Capi (the Bridge of the Four Heads) as it is decorated fore and aft by busts of two-faced Janus, the god of transitions and duality. The Pons Cestius is long gone, replaced during the Middle Ages. The Temple of Aesculapius has also gone, largely rebuilt into the Basilica of St Bartholomew, but medical succour is still available on the island in the form of a hospital manned by the Knights of St John, a Catholic order of military-style medics. The obelisk is still there, and in the Middle Ages the popes were in the habit of annually affixing on it the names of local ne'er-do-wells who were proscribed from Easter mass at the Vatican.

The Aemilian Bridge is now called the Ponte Rotto, the 'Broken Bridge'. Only the central span of Rome's oldest bridge remains, standing mid-river in defiance of the centuries.

The Forum Boarium is now a rather pleasant park, in which the temples of Portunus and Hercules still stand, in better shape now after recent restorations. Both temples remain by being converted into churches and thus surviving the vandalization visited upon purely 'pagan' monuments. An ancient circular carving of the face of the god Oceanus has also survived to be installed in the wall of a nearby church. Legend has it that anyone who inserts their hand into the open mouth of the god and tells a lie will get that hand bitten off. For this reason, the carving is today called the *Bocca della Verità* (the Mouth of Truth). Of Myron's famous sculpture, there is no sign.

The Baths of Sura survived into late antiquity but are now also gone, so the modern traveller might like to finish the day's walk at the very good Italian restaurant, The Apuleius, just around the corner.

REGIO X: THE CAPITOLINE AND PALATINE

Gods and Emperors

Today's walk takes us right into the very heart of imperial Rome. Note that if you are not very well connected and have not made the right arrangements beforehand, the middle part of this walk will have to be omitted. For obvious reasons the Roman emperors do not allow just anyone into the imperial palace on the Palatine Hill. Even if the emperors themselves are often not at home these days, the palace is a vital administrative centre where the functionaries have better things to do than accommodate gawking tourists. There's still a lot to see though, because most of the Capitoline Hill is open to visitors and the day's main attraction, the Circus Maximus, is not only open but can accommodate tens of thousands of visitors at a time – and regularly does.

The Capitoline Hill

Today's walk has a grim beginning. Start at the Temple of Concord in the forum and make your way uphill towards the top of the Capitoline by way of the infamous Gemonian steps. Assuming, that is, that the steps are not occupied. The authorities have the habit of leaving the corpses of executed criminals on these steps as a way of discouraging others of similar inclinations. Usually, the bodies are left to decompose to the point where feral dogs are no longer interested

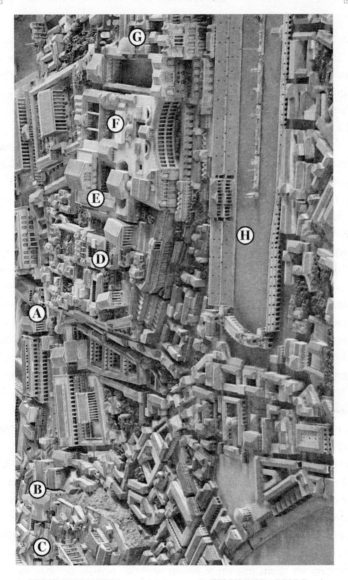

A FORUM ROMANUM   E TEMPLE OF APOLLO

B TEMPLE OF JUNO MONETA   F FLAVIAN PALACE

C TEMPLE OF JUPITER   G THE 'STADIUM'

D HOUSE OF AUGUSTUS   H CIRCUS MAXIMUS

in the remains, which are then gathered up and tossed into the Tiber.

If a corpse is displayed on the steps, this means that the executed individual was considered a public disgrace whose life should end in ignominy. That said, some distinguished individuals have perished here thanks to Rome's convoluted politics: one such victim was the Emperor Vitellius (mobbed on this spot in AD 69).

Generally speaking, if you are a Roman citizen, you don't end your life of crime in the arena. Slaves and foreigners might be executed as part of a public spectacle, but citizens tend to be quietly killed – generally by strangulation – in the prison built into the hillside up which the stairs run. This prison is the Tullianum, the main prison of Rome. At first glance this building seems absurdly small to serve as a prison for a city with a population that runs into the millions. In part that's because ordinary Romans are very proactive when it comes to criminality. Thieves and muggers end up getting lynched by an unsympathetic crowd at least as often as they are handed over to the authorities. Those who do end up in official custody don't stay there long. The Romans don't believe in incarceration as a punishment. So the Tullianum is where wrongdoers are put until they can be fined, flogged or executed. Turnover is brisk and no one stays there for long.

After leaving the dank confines of the prison, your view improves as you move uphill. Pause and enjoy the vista to the south when you are about 25 metres up the hill. The Capitoline is surrounded by steep cliffs on every side except the steps from the forum which you have just ascended. At this point the gentle incline stops and the drop to ground level is hereafter by way of a vertical cliff. This drop, the economically minded Romans of the Republic put to good use. Why hire an executioner when you can let gravity do the deed for free? So condemned criminals were hurled to their deaths from this point. The most frequent fliers were slaves condemned by their masters for theft, but those found guilty of perjury or of parricide can on occasion join the corpses at the bottom of this sheer drop.

There's a Roman saying, 'It's not far from the Capitol to the Tarpeian Rock', meaning that the downfall of those at the pinnacle of political life in Rome can be swift and very literal. (Although, in fact, the Tarpeian Rock is not much used these days – less because Rome has become more civilized than because of the inconvenience of needing to clear people from the busy space below before an execution and cleaning bits of people from the space after one.)

Almost below our feet is the roof of another building, in its own way another wonder of Rome. This is the Tabularium, the official record house of Rome. If someone proclaims *'Civis Romanus sum!'* ('I am a Roman citizen!'), a Tabularium is where they check that claim to citizenship. Built in the first century BC, this particular building is called 'the' Tabularium to distinguish it from lesser record offices scattered around Rome and the empire. Here military diplomas are displayed and records of manumission stored. Because this building is so tied to the functioning of the Roman state and religion is central to almost everything the Romans do, there is also a small temple contained within the building.

We are now upon the Capitoline itself – a hill that was settled long before Romulus made his home on the Palatine. The Capitoline is a hill with two peaks: the higher peak is the Arx to the north and the lower Capitolium is to the south. The saddle between the two is called 'Asylum'. Back in the days when he was desperate to build up Rome's manpower by any means possible, Romulus established a temple on Asylum. He decreed that anyone who could make it to the sanctuary there was safe from prosecution, no matter what the crime. On the Arx itself we come to an impressive temple, that of Juno Moneta ('Juno who gives warning', from the Latin verb *monere*, where we get the modern 'admonishment'). Most Roman temples are sturdy box-like establishments, but this temple of Juno takes it to extremes. In part that is because the temple was vowed to the goddess by the Roman general Camillus at a time when only the Capitol had (allegedly) withstood an assault by marauding Gauls when the rest of Rome had been conquered. Therefore, Camillus specified 'sturdy' as an architectural requirement for a building that might have to double as a fortress at short notice if the Gauls came back.

The temple was dedicated to Juno because a sneak attack on the Capitoline by those same Gauls was foiled when the geese sacred to

Juno sounded the alarm. (As any farmer can testify, if you have geese you don't need a watchdog.) Rome's last core of resistance was thus saved and Juno was rewarded with a temple.

The Story of Tarpeia

There's a long tradition of executions at this place. The very first was a Vestal Virgin called Tarpeia, although she was not crushed by a high-velocity fall. When Rome and the Sabines were at war, Tarpeia offered to let the Sabines into the fortifications on the Capitoline. In exchange she demanded that the Sabines gave her 'what they wore on their arms'. Tarpeia meant the golden torques and armbands that the warriors sported. The warriors took her more literally and, out of contempt for her treachery, they piled shields upon her until she was suffocated by the weight.

In later years, when the Roman mint was looking for a secure place to set up shop, the temple of Juno Moneta was the obvious choice. The location was secure, the walls sturdy and the Tullianum and Tarpeian Rock conveniently nearby for anyone who got too ambitious. As a result, the temple of Moneta has given the world the word 'money' and also – although the etymology is less certain – the word for mint.

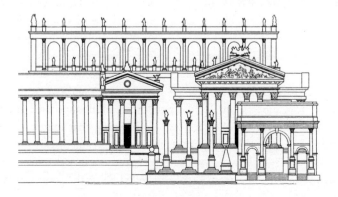

From here we move to another temple. Just as Romans refer to 'the' Tabularium despite the existence of other such offices around the city, when Romans refer to 'the' temple, there's only one place that they mean. That's the Aedes Iovis Optimi Maximi Capitolini – the Temple of Jupiter the Best and Greatest on the Capitolium. This name is actually wrong on at least two counts but there are 800 years of tradition behind it and the Romans are great sticklers for tradition, so that's the name it has got.

It is wrong because this is not actually a temple of Jupiter alone. It is a temple to the Capitoline Triad – the Gods Jupiter, Juno and Minerva. And any temple where these three gods are worshipped together is called a Capitolium – there's a good one in Hispania, for example. There is also a temple to Terminus, the god of boundaries, incorporated into the structure. While many shrines had to be moved to build the temple, Terminus made it plain by signs and auguries that he was not going anywhere. Since one does not want to offend The God Who Brings Things to an End, Terminus was left in place.

After all the compromises involved in the construction, it seems that the gods also became none too enamoured of this structure. It has had a turbulent existence, even without those times when it was blown out of existence by one of Jove's well-placed thunderbolts. Nevertheless, despite Jupiter's unsubtle hints, the Romans have stubbornly insisted on replacing the temple every time, and as masters of a great and growing empire they built back bigger and better with each iteration.

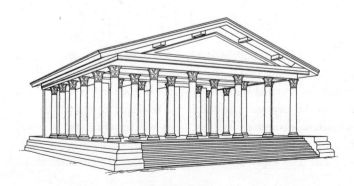

Getting Ahead in Early Rome

Excavations for the first temple on the hill began in the days of King Tarquin in the late sixth century BC. Work was paused when workers found a large detached head, apparently of a giant recently slain. This seemed rather ominous since there had been no giants around since the distant days of myth. Tarquin's soothsayers hastened to put a positive spin on things. The head, they explained, had been deposited by the gods to signify that one day Rome − centred on this very temple site − would become the capital of the world (the Latin for 'head' is *caput*).

To make sure everyone understood this interpretation, the hill (until then known as the Mons Saturnius) was renamed the Capitoline. Clearly either Tarquin's soothsayers were indeed blessed with great foresight, or the people who later concocted this legend had perfect hindsight as Rome did indeed go on to become the capital of the (known) world.

Another possible interpretation for the detached head might have been that Rome was about to lose its head of state − as it did soon thereafter in the revolution that deposed Tarquin and created the Roman Republic. The temple was formally dedicated in 509 BC by a Republican consul. Whichever prophecy you choose, note that if you ever wanted to stand at the religious centre of a continent-spanning empire, you've just reached your destination here at the Temple of Jupiter Capitolinus.

The first temple was built of wood, as was traditional for early Etruscan temples. It did not take long for Jupiter to demonstrate why building a temple of flammable materials on one of the most lightning-prone spots in the city was a bad idea. He managed to have the temple completely incinerated in 83 BC. This was an even greater disaster than just a devastating temple fire, because this blaze destroyed the prophetic texts called the Sibylline Books that the consuls had used to guide the state in previous times of crisis. The Romans did their best to replace these with pseudo-Sibylline Books from elsewhere in the empire, but things were never quite the same. One notes that the now poorly guided Republic crashed and burned soon thereafter in the series of civil wars that created the Roman empire.

The Romans persisted with the temple at this location, not least because for centuries the building on the Capitol was one of the grandest temples in all of Italy. The priests quickly figured out that well-earthed bronze statues on the roof were one way of making sure that the temple stayed unburned and (relatively) unzapped. Nevertheless, Jupiter smote the temple severely in 26 BC, in 9 BC and in AD 56.

When completely rebuilt, the temple was largely made of flame-proof marble, but nothing could be done about essential wooden structural parts such as roof beams. Being at the most defensible point in Rome meant that the temple was heavily involved in the civil war of AD 69 when it was burned down again. The winner of that civil war, the Flavian Emperor Vespasian, had the temple lavishly rebuilt, but hardly had the builders added the last lick of paint than the thing burned down again.

The final attempt was the work of Vespasian's son Domitian – this is the temple now on the site. It has lasted 300 years and counting. Looming over the forum as it does, this temple is the embodiment of the grandeur of Rome. The main columns are of rare white Pentelic marble, with supplementary columns made from the recast bronze rams of ships captured at the Battle of Actium in 31 BC. The doors are plated with gold and the roof is covered with gilt tiles. As ever with great Roman temples, statuary and great works of art stand within and on the temple grounds. Look particularly for a large equestrian bronze statue of the philosopher Emperor Marcus Aurelius located close to the front of the temple.

The Palatine

Because of those cliffs that make the Capitoline Hill so fine a defensive location, there's no easy way to get from the Capitoline to the Palatine Hill. Therefore, we must descend to the Forum Romanum along the route by which we came and look for the Domus Transitoria. As the name suggests, this is a sort of transit house. It was built by Nero to enable him to get from his palace on the Palatine (from which hill the word 'palace' is derived) to the gardens on the Pincian Hill while having minimal contact with Rome's unwashed plebs.

The once elaborate cryptoporticus (hidden gate) was severely mauled by the construction of the Baths of Trajan, but you can make your way through a nymphaeum (brutally remodelled with little regard to the original aesthetics) towards the Palatine. We arrive at the Domus Tiberiana, a palace built by the Emperor Tiberius (AD 14–37) before he abandoned Rome altogether for island life on Capri in the bay of Naples. Palace buildings of the early imperial era are relatively simple affairs uninfected with the grandiosity of Nero and later eras. 'Indeed,' remarks Suetonius in his biography of the Emperor Augustus, 'the furnishings of his palace … would have been considered mean and shabby even compared to an average town house today' (Suetonius, *Augustus* [71]).

These imperial residences are still sometimes open to the public and there are some glorious frescoes to be seen, particularly in the House of Livia. Livia, the wife of Augustus, is sometimes suspected of poisoning most of the Julian family, including her husband, in pursuit of her dynastic ends. Be that as it may, her rooms as well as her Portico near the Baths of Trajan show that the lady had superb taste – to the point where art lovers might be tempted to excuse her alleged forays into mass murder. *Vita brevis, ars longa*, as they say. ('Life is short, but art endures.')

From here we move on to the 'public' part of the imperial palace. This is the so-called Flavian Palace, because it was designed under the short-lived Emperor Titus and completed by his successor and younger brother Domitian. The Flavian emperors were keen to show their subjects that, unlike the self-indulgent Julio-Claudians whom they had replaced, their rule was all about public service. So this 'palace' is basically a set of offices designed so efficiently that subsequent emperors have not seen the need to make any but minor cosmetic changes.

The poet Martial described the work in one of his *Epigrams* (7.56) in which he praises Domitian's architect Rabirius:

> *You had the stars of the heavens in your pious mind, Rabirius*
> *When with marvellous skill you built this house.*

The room that has seen the most alterations is the Aula Regia – sometimes called the 'throne room'. This is where the emperor meets with foreign dignitaries and petitioners when he is in Rome. The whole point of the throne room is to get ambassadors and petitioners into a suitably humble frame of mind through the sheer size and grandeur of the place. The poet Statius went into raptures about it:

> *Wider than an outspread plain are the foundations of the halls*
> *While the roof embraces the heavens*
> *Here stone from the mountains of Libya*
> *Competes in beauty with the bright stone of Troy*

And graven blocks from Cyrene.
From Chios comes stone to mirror the grey-green sea.
From Carystos, marble, and also from Luna
For columns so high that straining eyes
Barely see the ceiling, imagining it instead
To be the golden vault of heaven.

Statius, *Silvae* (4.2)

When we strip out the poetic license, we end up with a hall some 30 metres across and 50 long, magnificently adorned with dark red and coffee-coloured stone with an apse at the end, so that visitors must pass through the entire imposing hallway to meet the emperor enthroned. The roof is indeed lofty, enough to accommodate another three levels had the designers not been out to impress. As it is, the height of the ceiling dwarfs the colossal statues that line the walls, staring down at visitors crossing the wide marble expanse and making them feel – exactly as intended – small and puny by comparison.

It comes as a relief to exit into the peristyle garden, a pleasantly open space – although Domitian had the pillars on this peristyle polished to mirror brightness so that he could spot any potential assassins creeping up behind him. Beyond the peristyle you cannot venture because these are the imperial family's private quarters. Those burly figures lurking by the bushes are not there to admire the flowers, as you will painfully discover if you even appear to be contemplating an illegal entry. In fact, the emperor's praetorian guard have a room up one of the stairways leading from this peristyle – a room into which you do not want to be dragged.

Instead, while attempting to radiate innocence, quickly move westwards to where the Palatine's close-packed buildings open on to a magnificent balcony that is the best place in Rome from which to view the chariot races in the Circus Maximus located in the valley below. There's a highly incongruous hut here – considerably less imposing than a gardener's shed.

As written in *c.* 10 BC:

> [It is] *a mountain hut made of sticks and reeds – even the roof.*
> *Even in my own time this stands on the slope of the Palatine,*
> *looking toward the Circus. It is maintained like a shrine, but*
> *never embellished. If time or weather damages anything, it is*
> *repaired, but in a manner that restores it as closely as possible to*
> *the original.*

> Dionysius of Halicarnassus, *Roman Antiquities* (1.79)

This is alleged to be the home of the first ruler of Rome – Romulus himself is believed to have lived in this hut, which is preserved as a way for the Romans to congratulate themselves on how far they have come since then.

Further down the hill, almost directly below the House of Augustus, you'll come to a large cult statue that stands in front of a richly decorated grotto extending some 15 metres into the hillside. It's a very elaborate setting – not at all what one would expect of a wolf's den. However, the place must have looked very different 1,000 years ago when a she-wolf who had lost her cubs found a pair of abandoned human babies to relieve the pressure in her aching dugs. This is the cave of the Lupercal, where Romulus and Remus were reared until they were discovered by the shepherd Faustulus. Every year, ceremonies ritually purifying the city begin at this location. Since the Latin for purification by purging is *februare*, it is not hard to guess in which month the ceremonies take place.

Winding back uphill the path takes us to the Temple of the Great Mother, the Magna Mater. This is the goddess Cybele who is worshipped in the form of a large stone that fell from the heavens. For a while, a nearby temple of Jupiter was dedicated by the Emperor Elagabalus to another such stone. Once Elagabalus was killed in AD 218, this stone was shipped back to its original temple in Emesa in Anatolia. Cybele is still very much present, and Romans regard with fascinated horror her priests, who are known as Galli. These priests are eunuchs because they castrate themselves in dedication to their

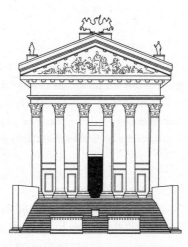

goddess. Romans don't participate much in the rites of Cybele, but they regard her as important for the harvest and the fertility of the population. In fact, it was partly to avert population decline in the third century BC that the Romans imported the goddess Cybele on advice from the (now incinerated) Sibylline Books.

One does not always need oracular texts to advise on when and where to build a temple. The god Apollo made that clear to the Emperor Augustus when he personally indicated where he would like a temple built to himself by blasting the area clear with a lightning bolt. Augustus obediently built a sumptuous temple on the location. This elegant Temple of Apollo of the Palatine overlooks the Circus Maximus, so racegoers can look up at the imperial houses on the Palatine and see looming above them literal concrete (and marble) proof of their emperor's piety. As well as a magnificent set of statues of Apollo and his twin sister Diana, other priceless sculptures stand behind the ivory doors to the premises.

However, for those with a certain mindset, of far greater value are the books that generations of emperors have gathered in the Palatine Library adjoining the temple. These include the new generation of Sibylline texts that Augustus, as chief priest of Rome, removed from their evidently perilous premises on the Capitoline and stashed here, safely close at hand.

Second-hand Luxury

As well as a floor of fine mosaic, the walls of the Palatine banqueting hall are a riot of marble in yellow, red, white, green and grey. Sad to say though, much of this magnificence is second-hand. It was originally part of the Palatine extension of Nero's Golden House. When that affront to the common people of Rome was demolished after Nero's downfall, it seemed to the frugal Flavians a pity that these extravagant marbles should go to waste. Therefore the tiles, mosaics and carvings were incorporated into the banqueting hall, creating the impression of imperial opulence at minimal cost.

A passage from the Temple of Apollo takes us back to the Flavian Palace and the last room on our Palatine tour. This is the banqueting hall. When you imagine Neronian orgies or Caligulan debauchery, it is in rooms such as this where they would have happened. Regrettably or otherwise, such events seldom, if ever, take place in reality, but the banqueting hall certainly represents the ultimate venue for fine dining – and in a room comparable in size to the imposing Throne Room nearby (the banqueting hall is larger but lower). The windows look out onto the flowers and fountains of the peristyle, while a system of heating by hypocaust ensures that temperatures remain mild even in the depths of winter.

The Circus Maximus

From the Flavian Palace make your way downhill to the Murcian Valley, a space some 300 metres wide that lies between the Palatine and Aventine Hills. Murcia is a divinity from the time of pre-Roman settlement in the area, a goddess so ancient that no one is now sure who she is or what she does. Nevertheless, just to be on the safe side, her ancient altar is preserved on the site, unhelpfully known as the *ara vetus* (ancient altar).

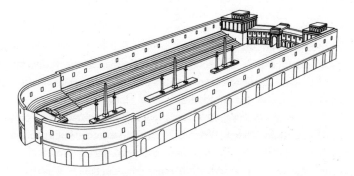

From the time of the founding, the Romans used this open grassy space for sports and horse races. It is believed that this is where Romulus once invited the Sabines to attend a family outdoor event. That led to the infamous Rape of the Sabine Women, which began with the Romans abducting every unmarried female that they could lay their hands on.

Once the ructions from this atrocity had finally been resolved – traditionally through the mediation of the kidnapped women themselves – the Romans began holding chariot races at this location in honour of another ancient god, Consus. Consus was a god of the harvest and the Underworld. In later centuries his portfolio has largely been taken over by the greater god Saturn, and Consus has few places of worship remaining other than a shrine at the racetrack. (While the Romans are quite at ease with retiring gods for whom they have no further need, they never ditch them entirely, just in case.)

In the early days, races were very much a seasonal event because the valley became a marsh in spring when the stream that flowed down from the Caelian Hill joined with floods from the Tiber. It was only when Roman engineering reached the point where the stream could be converted to an underground channel that a permanent racetrack could be developed.

The important bit of a chariot racetrack is the *spina*. Unlike horse races which go from A to B, horses pulling racing chariots gallop around a tight oval track for a defined number of circuits – usually seven. The *spina* is there as a dividing barrier so that horses going south-east on the outwards loop don't run into those chariots going in the opposite direction on the north-western part of the circuit. To count the circuits, large wooden balls (called *ova* or 'eggs') were placed on what we'll have to call egg cups on the *spina*, so spectators could quickly count the empty egg cups to keep track of how many circuits the racers had completed.

To make counting even easier the chief henchman of Augustus, Marcus Agrippa, added golden dolphins (a salute to Augustus' naval victory at the Battle of Actium) that dipped their heads with each completed lap. For a dash of the esoteric, Augustus added to the number of obelisks which the Romans were in the habit of looting from Egypt and positioning around the city. This obelisk he added to the decorations on the *spina*. This particular obelisk was selected from the Egyptian city of Heliopolis because that city was dedicated to the sun god, as was the Circus Maximus as a whole. (Another obelisk was added later.) People watched the races while picnicking on the hillsides until Julius Caesar formalized the situation by adding proper seating – which, in fine Roman tradition, promptly burned down.

The Circus you see today was given its form by the Emperor Trajan who sensibly made the lower level of seating of stone. Two wooden upper levels have built up capacity to the point where the Circus can accommodate a reasonable percentage of the entire population of the city at one time. Because the Romans don't mind getting crowded together to an almost illogical degree, a really popular racecard can see up to a quarter of a million people crammed on to the stands of the Circus itself (Pliny, *Natural History* [36.102]), with free viewing still available from the slopes of the Aventine. (Seating on the Palatine is these days reserved for a small and very exclusive group.)

*The enormous – excuse me if I say 'excessive' – population of
     Rome is at the Circus
The crowd's roar beats upon the ear, so I deduce the Greens
     have won
If they'd lost the city would have been appalled and silent,
As though the consuls lay defeated once again in the dust at
     Cannae.*

Well let the young men watch; they like the clamour, the
*   bold bets –*
And sitting beside a pretty girl.

Juvenal, *Satires* (11.200ff)

There are four teams that compete in the races. (Juvenal was evidently a fan of the Greens, as was the Emperor Caligula.) The others were the Reds, the Blues and the Whites. Supporters of each of the teams get genuinely fanatical about the result, to the extent where the urban cohorts have to be on alert for serious rioting if one faction or another feels they were unfairly deprived of a win. Charioteers make obscene amounts of money in return for taking the extreme risks inherent in the sport. They literally live fast and die young – to the extreme grief of their devoted followers. 'When Felix, a charioteer of the Reds, was being cremated, one of his admirers threw himself upon the funeral pyre in an act of total stupidity' (Pliny the Elder, *Natural History* [7.54]).

The Circus is the largest single structure in Rome, being over 600 metres long and 120 metres wide. The outside of the Circus has street-facing rows of shops built under the seats. These are a notoriously seedy selection of drinking dens, dodgy fast-food joints, gimcrack souvenir stalls and nooks that prostitutes rent by the hour.

The Original Circus

Because the Circus can hold around three times the size of the crowd in the amphitheatre in the Colosseum, sometimes the emperors stage events here to entertain the masses – and make themselves more popular with them. Such events might be gladiator fights, wild beast displays, acrobats or the ingeniously sadistic execution of criminals. It is these extra-curricular activities (apart from the executions) that will become what later generations expect to see at a 'circus'.

Entry to the Circus is through a triple arch, which, like the arch on the Velia, was built by Titus to celebrate his victories in the Judean war. On race day the magistrates, priests and entertainers, as well as such senators as are attending, parade through this arch. There's also a special box called the *pulvinar* from where the emperor can watch the races if he wants a view closer than that afforded from his home on the Palatine.

Finish today's walk by heading right across the valley and up the Aventine for a soak in the Baths of Decius. Unlike the Baths of Caracalla over the hill, these baths are not a mass-production facility for churning out freshly washed Romans but a more exclusive affair catering to the more sophisticated and aristocratic denizens of the Aventine. Given the limited clientele, the Baths of Decius are substantial – about 70 by 30 metres – which gives bathers plenty of elbow room. The rooms are tastefully decorated with works of art such as the infant Hercules in green basalt and a relief depicting the story of Endymion. Overall, then, the Baths of Decius give the sort of bathing experience one should expect after spending a day on the rarefied heights of the Palatine.

THE TWENTY-FIRST CENTURY WALK

You can still get from the forum to the Capitoline by way of the Tullianum, but these days the prison is called the Mamertine, because a temple of Mars was believed to stand nearby. Your fellow visitors will include a large Christian contingent, because St Peter was incarcerated here before his execution. As a result, the former prison has become a chapel, and there's a stubborn belief that the spring in the lower level of the prison, er, sprang miraculously into being so that Peter could baptise his fellow prisoners. (The Church authorities rather irritably point out that the spring was well attested before St Peter's time.)

The Capitoline Hill, *Il Campidoglio* to modern Romans, has changed beyond all recognition since the fifth century. And not necessarily for the worse. The Asylum is gone, although thousands of people all around the world still seek it every year. Where the Asylum once stood, there's now a splendid piazza designed by Michelangelo and the equestrian statue of Marcus Aurelius is a prominent feature. This is an exact copy. The original is now in the nearby Capitoline Museum. It is the only equestrian bronze statue to have survived from antiquity and the authorities would like it to be around for a little longer.

Thanks to Michelangelo, you can also access the Capitoline by way of a staircase of his design that climbs up the hill from Piazza d'Aracoeli beside the Piazza Venezia. The Tabularium was another victim of Michelangelo and has now become the rather elegant Palazzo Senatorio. Look also for the iconic statue of the she-wolf suckling Romulus and Remus. This is again a replica. The original is, once more, in the Capitoline Museum. Note that the she-wolf is an Etruscan sculpture and the twins were added over a thousand years later by a Renaissance artist.

It's practically compulsory to visit the museum here, where many of the artworks that once graced buildings in Rome have been gathered into this one spot. This includes the infant Hercules in green basalt and the Endymion bas-relief that were once seen in the Baths of Decius. This rather compensates for the fact that all that remains of the Temples of Jupiter and Juno are today rather forlorn archaeological sites largely ignored by the bustling mass of tourists.

The Palatine retains barely a shadow of its former self. It might have been these ruins that inspired the Victorian poet Tennyson to write in his *Ode to Virgil*: 'Now thy Forum roars no longer, / fallen, every purple Caesar's dome.' (This is not actually correct – the dome of Hadrian's Pantheon hasn't fallen. In fact, it remains the largest unsupported concrete dome in the world.) If we are thinking of the Aula Regia, the Temple of Apollo or the imperial banqueting hall, 'fallen' only begins to describe their condition. It takes a lot of imagination to reconstruct past glories from these scattered lumps of masonry.

Parts of the Flavian Palace are still standing, including the gardens, which have somehow picked up the name of 'the Hippodrome', though there is scant evidence that any equestrian events ever happened here. The House of Livia is perhaps the surviving building in the best condition, and the remnants of the frescoes on the walls give us a glimpse of their vanished beauty. The Palace of Tiberius has gone entirely, replaced by the Farnese Gardens. These were laid out in the early Renaissance and are some of Europe's oldest botanical gardens.

Much of what remains of the imperial Palatine has been gathered into the Palatine Museum where the frescoes, mosaics and objets d'art are a reminder of the hill's vanished glories.

If today's Palatine would have been unrecognizable to Domitian and his successors, the Circus Maximus would be instantly recognizable to a reincarnated Romulus. The massive edifice of Trajan has gone almost without a trace and in its place is an elongated grassy valley that cries out for the same horse races and sporting events that took place there almost 3,000 years ago. Of the two obelisks once adorning the spina, one can be seen today in the centre of Piazza del Popolo and the other outside the Lateran Basilica, the latter being one of the oldest and most beautiful churches in Rome.

Today, the area formerly occupied by the Circus is a valued green space in the heart of the city, easily accessible from the Metro stop handily named the Circo Massimo. Romans and visitors alike picnic here, confident that the atrocity of the Sabine women is unlikely to be perpetrated by the city's modern inhabitants.

The modern walk should stop with a picnic basket here at the Circo Massimo, for the Baths of Decius are no more. The foundations lie partly under the Piazza del Tempio di Diana, with some remains in the basement of the adjoining mansion of the Casale Torlonia.

REGIO XIV: TRANSTIBERIM AND THE VATICAN

Rome across the Tiber

There's not a lot to research about the Transtiberim district, even though it's one of the largest residential areas in Rome. The area lacks the louche reputation of the Subura without the distinction of being inhabited by the gentry. When upper-class Romans (which includes almost every Roman with the leisure to write or the means to buy lots of writing material) do talk of Transtiberim, it is mostly to complain about the whiff from the city tanneries that are largely situated on the west bank of the Tiber. Tanneries are forbidden to operate within the *pomerium*.

The attitude of those east of the Tiber towards the folk of Transtiberim is a sort of absent-minded contempt. The poet Horace nicely summed up this attitude when he describes wines from the Janiculum Hill (which bounds Transtiberim to the east) as 'the sort of stuff you drink when you can't get vinegar'. Nevertheless, for the average Roman, Transtiberim has a lot going for it. There are some pleasant, unpretentious parks, the streets are wider, and the houses are roomier and cheaper than on the east side of the river. Also, if you do not make a career out of visiting the great monuments of the city, you can do well with Transtiberim's share of ordinary eateries, taverns and markets.

Today's walk starts at the foot of the Aventine Hill at the Sublician Bridge. In an ideal world the walk would begin somewhat further to

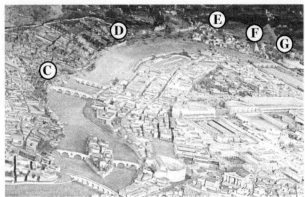

Map has been split in two for clarity; label C appears twice to show the overlap.

A PORTA PORTUENSIS   E CIRCUS OF NERO
B JANICULAN MILLS   F PYRAMID TOMB
C JANICULAN FORT   G MAUSOLEUM OF HADRIAN
D PORTA SETTIMANA

the south, but no one has got around to bridging the Tiber any further downstream, so those living near the Gardens of (Julius) Caesar have a long daily commute if their business takes them across the Tiber.

Avoiding Cleopatra

Those wandering down the urban stretch of the Via Portuensis between Caesar's Gardens and the Tiber may reflect that Caesar's *amoratrix*, Cleopatra of Egypt, probably walked this same stretch of road when she came to Rome to remind Caesar of his obligations towards the son they had together. Being a royal, Cleopatra was by ancient custom forbidden to enter the *pomerium*, which had been proscribed to kings and queens since the time of Tarquin. Caesar, who had faced down pirates, charging Gauls, Germans and even Roman legionaries, thereafter spent an unconscionable amount of time safely out of Cleopatra's reach within the *pomerium*.

Walk as far as the first milestone on the Via Portuensis where there is an ancient shrine to Fortuna, which was established by Servius Tullius, the sixth king of Rome. It is instructive to compare the ancient style of the bronze statues at this shrine with the much more fluid and lifelike marble and bronze works in the city centre. Proceed northwards along the slopes of the Janiculum, the long ridge of which marks the informal western edge of the city. Re-enter the enclosed section of the city again via the Porta Portuensis, a standard city gate flanked by two circular towers.

(Although the Aurelian Walls make a sporting attempt to enclose part of Transtiberim, most of this district is outside the walls – the area is just too large to enclose, and by the Roman system of values there's no one and nothing of great importance to protect anyway.)

There's little to interrupt a pleasant walk except to take a break alongside Hercules, whose statue is doing the same at the shrine called

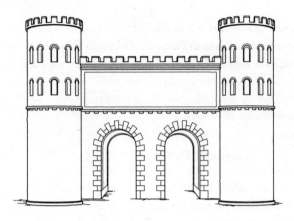

Hercules Cubans. (Nothing to do with the Caribbean isle, *cubans* in Latin is a participle meaning 'reclining'.) Somewhere around here is the site of the famed *naumachia* of the early Caesars. These were basically large hollows filled with water and used to entertain the Romans with mock naval battles (which were all too real for the condemned men forced to fight in them). Julius Caesar staged one of these battles, as did Augustus, who never lost an opportunity to remind the public of his epic victory at the naval Battle of Actium. These days, *naumachia* are no longer staged, not least because the available land has been comprehensively built over in the centuries since.

Near the top of the Janiculum, near where the Triana Aqueduct enters the city, you'll find a busy complex taking advantage of the downwards impetus of gravity to force the water into a complex of water-powered mills that grind much of the city's grain. Providing for Rome's vast population distorts not just the local agricultural market, but the agricultural economics of places as far away as Carthage and other cities in north Africa and Alexandria in Egypt.

From the Janiculum's light industrial zone make your way to the Janiculan Citadel. This stands on a prominence on the Janiculan ridge and has for almost 1,000 years been the city's westernmost point of defence against attack. If we are to believe the writer Dionysius of Halicarnassus, the site is much older than even this early date, being the fort of a settlement founded directly by the son of Aeneas.

> *Aeneia which was afterwards called the Janiculum ... was*
> *for some time deserted, but upon the arrival of another colony,*
> *which the people of Alba Longa sent out under the leadership*
> *of Romulus and Remus, the ancient name was revived again.*
> *Therefore by this telling there were two settlements of Rome,*
> *one just after the Trojan war, and the other fifteen generations*
> *later.*
>
> Dionysius of Halicarnassus, *Roman Antiquities* (1.73)

Leave the defended part of the city by way of the strangely named Porta Settimiana. No one is sure where the name (or the gate also) comes from. Some believe it was originally part of an ancient fort defending the northern approach to the Aemilian Bridge. Others claim that it was built by Geta, a son of the Emperor Septimius Severus, which makes sense as Geta's gardens and palace lie just to the west. There's an interesting copse of trees here, nearer to the walls than the Romans usually allow. However, this copse is sacred to the Furies, those dread avenging beings of myth, and it would be a brave man who ordered their destruction. Here, by tradition, is where the reforming Tribune Gaius Gracchus met his death, persecuted by the reactionary senators of the late Republic.

Over the river the buildings of the Campus Martius will now be visible, meaning that in this prolonged ramble you have covered about half the length of the city from north to south, a walk of around 4 kilometres. The Vatican Hill is on the left, awaiting your attention this afternoon, but for now pass between the hill and the Tiber to view one of the most imposing burial sites in the entire city. This is the Mausoleum of Hadrian.

Hadrian's Mausoleum

The Emperor Hadrian (AD 117–38) built a wall running from one side of the island of Britain to the other. He was not a man to think small, so it comes as no surprise that he took the same approach when it came to his burial place. Apart from the even more flamboyant efforts of the Egyptian pharaohs, few tombs are as imposing. The drum-shaped main body of the tomb stands 21 metres high – and that's on top of a raised rectangular base and without counting the imposing statue on the top. So large is it that this monument will have been visible for much of the morning, starting from the uphill climb to the Janiculan Citadel and looming ever larger as you proceed northwards.

The tomb stands beside the Tiber in the relaxing setting of the Gardens of Domitia (the Domitia in question being Domitia Longina, the wife of the Emperor Domitian). These gardens became all the more popular with Romans looking to escape the heat of the city after Hadrian had a bridge constructed across the Tiber to facilitate access to the mausoleum. This is the Pons Aelius, 'Aelius' being the *gentilicium* (family name) of Hadrian. Being this close to the tomb, you have to strain your neck to see the gigantic four-horse chariot from which the effigy of the late emperor gazes down upon Rome.

Hadrian has quite the view from up there – and indeed even the views from the levels below the statue are reputed to be among the best in Rome. From here you can see the dome of the Pantheon, most distinctive of the buildings on the Campus Martius (which include the comparatively puny tomb of Augustus), the racetrack of Domitian, the looming bulk of the Theatre of Pompey and all the way past the Tiber Island.

In his defence, Hadrian did not intend this extremely commodious resting place for himself alone. In fact, the original intention was to create a suitable place to inter the remains of Nerva – Hadrian's predecessor but one. Trajan, the immediate predecessor of Hadrian, was buried under the eponymous column in his forum, but there had been something of a question about what to do with Nerva. The original imperial tomb (the Mausoleum of Augustus) was so packed that cramming in another set of remains would be an affront to imperial dignity, and Hadrian himself needed a decent resting place, as did his successors. Hence the new mausoleum. Apart from Nerva, the first occupants of the tomb were Hadrian's adopted son, his wife, and Hadrian himself. This has left space for emperors well

into the foreseeable future, especially as cremation was favoured in Hadrian's day and the twenty or so funeral urns that the monument contains take up only a miniscule fraction of the space.

In any case, the procession of emperors into the sepulchre ended eighty years later with Caracalla in AD 217. Later Roman emperors tend either to prefer their own customized tombs or to have died messily and unlamented too far from Rome to be worth transporting there. (For example, there is a well-stocked imperial mausoleum in Milan in north Italy.) Nevertheless, the tomb remains with rooms vacant should any future emperor decide to spend eternity in Hadrian's company.

The monument is walled off, so to approach you need to begin at the Aelian Bridge and go down a walkway lined with pillars topped with bronze peacocks. There's a slope that leads to the garden-like area at the top of the rectangular base. Much of the space is taken up by the huge drum of the main tower, which is 68 metres across, but there is a profusion of statuary adorning this base that is low enough for the art to be admired by passers-by at ground level.

This base is built from brick faced with Rome's trusty travertine stone, but the main part of the edifice – the drum – is gleaming Parian marble wrapped around a concrete core. Were you to enter this part of the building you would first behold the face of Hadrian himself atop a larger-than-life marble statue, with an equally substantial statue of Hadrian's successor Antoninus Pius standing beside him. From there a spiral ramp, thoughtfully shaped to accommodate funeral cortèges, winds its way up to the central chamber where the funeral vases are actually kept. Should any mourners want to keep going up and enjoy the view while they are there, the way continues (although now a much-diminished staircase) to the top.

The Vatican Hill

After relaxing in the shade of the trees in the Garden of Domitia, it's time to gird your loins and head up the Vatican Hill. Again, if the sacred number of hills required for Rome had been eight, then the Vatican might have been roped in. But as the number was seven and several of the bulges of the Esquiline ridge have been redesignated as hills to reach that number, the Vatican Hill does not count as one of the seven hills of Rome, although it is part of the Transtiberim region.

There's a pleasant colonnaded terrace near the hilltop with views over the city. This terrace is part of another set of gardens named, as are the Gardens of Domitia down the hill, after an imperial lady. These are the Gardens of Agrippina, the woman perhaps best known today as the mother of Caligula and grandmother of Nero. Agrippina was not just unfortunate in the matter of her family members but also fell victim to the vicious politics of the later Julio-Claudian era. Ultimately, she was exiled from Rome and her guards made sure that she died in AD 33 of starvation on the prison island of Pandateria. The manner of his mother's death may have contributed to the jaundiced outlook on life of her son Caligula who built a racetrack in these gardens when he inherited them.

To this racetrack, the Emperor Claudius – probably in imitation of Augustus – added an obelisk from Heliopolis in Egypt, just as Augustus had added one of these obelisks to the *spina* of the Circus Maximus. The Vatican's obelisk is of red sandstone and stands over 25 metres high – in fact, so large is this obelisk that the ship that brought it to Rome was custom-built for the purpose.

Agrippina's grandson Nero not only embellished this racetrack but scandalized Rome while he was about it:

> *He took a fancy for driving the chariot himself, and he even did so publicly. He first tried his skills in the Gardens* [of Agrippina], *watched by crowds of slaves and other low-lifes. Eventually though, he did this for everyone to see in the Circus Maximus.*

Suetonius, Nero (22)

Charioteers, Imperial and Otherwise

When Nero's enemies rose against him in rebellion, one of the many insults they hurled at him was that he was a 'charioteer'. These men had something of a reputation in Rome – they were immensely rich and popular and if some of the more lurid allegations against them are correct, they could literally get away with murder. The authorities have reined in these excesses but such conduct is understandable, if not excusable, from men who felt that they had little to lose. The Circus Maximus was and is a very dangerous place for those on the track. There are few rules to protect the safety of the drivers and pile-ups were common. The charioteers secured the reins around their waists to keep their hands free for control of their horses and vehicle. If a chariot overturned or the driver fell out, he was dragged at speed by his overexcited horses amid a lethal chaos of chariot wheels. Men that careless of their personal safety tended to also have little regard for social convention – and in his disdain for public opinion, Nero did have that much in common with them.

After the Great Fire that burned down much of Rome in AD 64, suspicion arose that Nero's agents had set the fire themselves as a form of drastic urban clearance to make room for the emperor's planned Golden House. To deflect suspicion, Nero cast blame on another group whom the Romans regarded with equal wariness: the Christians. Once again, the Gardens of Agrippina were the venue in which Nero indulged his unseemly conduct. (The Circus Maximus was among the structures damaged by the fire and so was unavailable.) The historian Tacitus, who was a youth when these events took place, describes the events in the Gardens of Agrippina with deep distaste:

> *The Christians were generally hated for their conduct, so Nero charged them with the guilt attributed to himself by rumour ... those first arrested and who confessed to being Christians in turn gave up others until a multitude of people were condemned, not so much for burning the city as for warring upon the human race.*
>
> *Their deaths were made a kind of sport. Some were dressed in the hides of wild animals and torn to death by dogs and others were crucified. When the daylight faded they were burned alive to serve as lighting for the evening. Nero's own gardens were used for the spectacle, with Nero mingling with the common folk in the crowd while dressed as a charioteer or standing in an actual chariot.*

> Tacitus, *Annals* (15.44)

The most famous of Nero's victims was the chief of Christ's followers, St Peter. There is an enduring dispute over whether Peter was executed in the Neronian purge that followed the fire or considerably later in AD 67. It is undisputed, though, that his death was by crucifixion on the Vatican Hill, and the most accepted account is that this was done *inter* (between) *duas metas*. The two *metas* (goals/points of reference) in question are somewhat more problematic. One of them is definitely the 'Vatican pyramid' (a counterpart to the Pyramid of Cestius). This pyramid was probably built at the height of a previous generation's fascination with Egypt. It can still be seen near the Via Triumphalis, covered with fine marble with a 6.5 metre open space around. This space is floored with travertine stone with its own drainage gutter and garden.

The other point of reference is unknown. It might have been a large terebinth tree. This might be the tree later called 'Nero's obelisk', although that name is also given to one of the many funerary memorials in this area. (The Vatican Hill has been used as a necropolis since pre-Roman times.) Anyway, St Peter was laid to rest by the tree, near the intersection of the Via Cornelia and the Via Triumphalis, and the site of his death immediately became a place of pilgrimage for Rome's Christian community. In fact, the bishops of Rome have taken up residence near this burial site, which is on the eastern side of the hill with the gardens and hilltop behind. Over the centuries, this residence and accompanying church have grown ever grander – a process that shows no sign of stopping.

From here, bypass the undistinguished shrine to the Magna Mater and proceed to the most north-westerly point on this Roman tour to view the Vatican Naumachia, also sometimes mistakenly referred to as the 'Circus of Hadrian'. While the site of the Augustan *naumachia* is now built over, this building still survives due to being right on the outskirts of the city. The somewhat derelict stadium is now dilapidated and no mock naval battles have happened here for centuries. But it is possible to stand and look down at the muddy soil in the central space, 36,000 metres square, and imagine it as a

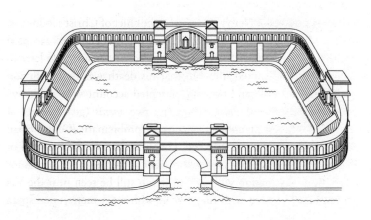

mini lake filled with water while a bloodthirsty crowd cheered on the combatants from the tiers of seating that surrounded it.

There are no decent public baths on the Vatican Hill, so to finish the day one must go downhill and over the Aelian Bridge. There, if you can still stomach being associated with the man's memory, you will find the Baths of Nero, 100 metres down the road. It helps that these baths are not now the sumptuously decadent baths built by Nero. The place was renovated and basically rebuilt by the Emperor Alexander Severus in AD 228 and is now the largest public baths in the northern part of Rome. After a cooling dip in the north-facing tepidarium, enjoy the warm waters in the caldarium and indulge in a massage in the evening sunlight. All around are the buildings of the Campus Martius, where tomorrow's walk will tour this final part of the ancient city.

THE TWENTY-FIRST CENTURY WALK

Today there are many reasons for visiting the Transtiberim region, which now goes under the name of Trastevere. The place has a bohemian atmosphere, offers excellent dining and is away from the general tourist crush. However, if the purpose of your visit is to rediscover the remains of the ancient city, Trastevere has little to offer.

Much of the area is now composed of those solid apartment blocks that are the modern Roman equivalent of the ancient *insulae*, and in the early afternoon (the time the locals call the *controra*), the place feels almost like a ghost town. Wait until the early evening, though, and Trastevere comes alive. The coffee shops, bars and restaurants open up as the region gets on with what it has been doing for thousands of years: accommodating the needs of working Romans without showiness or fuss.

Therefore, today's walk is best done in reverse order to the ancient walk – start by the monumental buildings to the north-west and when you are sated with art and statuary, take the twenty-minute stroll from the Vatican to Trastevere and, once there, relax for the evening.

When transiting from the Vatican to Trastevere, take care to go by the Via della Lungara. That way you will do as generations have done before you and enter by way of the Porta Settimiana, which looks as good as ever it did. Sadly the gate's twin to the south, the Porta Portuensis, is no more. In contrast to their cavalier attitude to most ancient monuments, generations of popes have maintained or embellished the Settemiana gate partly because it once had a defensive function (before Pope Urban VIII tore down the Aurelian Walls) and later because it was a useful toll booth on the Sacred Way by which pilgrims approached the Vatican from the south.

There's not much to see of the watermills that once operated on the Janiculum, although they were in operation for centuries after the fall of the Roman empire. Today, there is usually a contingent of archaeologists on the site working at understanding how exactly these mills operated. It's worth the walk though, not just to view the remnants of the Aqua Traiana but also because this location offers some of the best views of the city of Rome as a whole.

Hadrian's tomb is still there and as magnificent as ever, although now it's known by its modern alias of the Castel Sant'Angelo. The 'angel' in question is the Archangel Michael whose monumental statue has replaced that of Hadrian atop the building. When Rome was being devastated by a plague in the late sixth century, Pope Gregory had a vision of the avenging angel sheathing his sword above the building as a sign the city's travails were coming to an end, so the castle has been associated with Michael ever since.

The 'Castel' part of the name goes back even earlier, since in the troubled times after the fall of the empire it didn't take people long to work out that the large, raised wall had considerable defensive potential, especially with an insurmountable stone building perched atop that.

Due to its proximity to the Vatican, the Castel has served the popes as a bolthole in unexpected emergencies, a papal fortress, a barracks and a prison. The ashes of Hadrian and other deceased members of the imperial family have vanished somewhere along the way (probably during the Visigothic sack of Rome in AD 410), and the site is now open to anyone who can afford the modest entrance fee. It is worth it just to enjoy the view from the upper level and to contemplate the scene of one of the most famous suicides in opera: it was from the ramparts of the Castel Sant'Angelo that Verdi's heroine Tosca threw herself after the death of her lover by firing squad at this same location.

The Vatican is now synonymous with the huge basilica that dominates the hill. Technically this is not part of Rome per se, or indeed part of Italy itself, since the Vatican City is a separate state. Nevertheless, passport checks are not part of a visit, and visitors with an interest in history really do need to see the Vatican Museums while they are in Rome. Here many of the remnants of the ancient city have been gathered in one place. These are statues, mosaics and frescoes, while anyone with an interest in forensic archaeology can also derive morbid pleasure from prowling the building and attempting to establish which bits of classical Rome's great monuments ended up in which walls. It is not hard, for example, to determine the provenance of the red sandstone obelisk that towers over the entrance to St Peter's Square: that's the one Claudius imported to decorate the *spina* of the racetrack that once stood nearby.

The Vatican Museums – rated as among the world's most important – are themselves precious cultural artefacts apart from the many treasures contained within. Open to the public since the sixteenth century, they now receive 6 to 8 million visitors every year. Another reason for starting the modern walk at this location is because in the tourist season the line to enter the premises stretches back for a considerable distance and it may be necessary to modify your day's plans depending on the length of your Vatican sojourn.

Should you decide to bail out of the line, take the time saved to stroll downhill to the Aelian Bridge over the Tiber. This other enduring contribution of Hadrian to the city remains not only intact, but considerably embellished. As an added bonus, the city authorities no longer display the rotting corpses of executed criminals at the foot of the bridge. As it is only for pedestrian use, distractions from admiring the bridge's artistic stonework are few.

When the bridge was the main route by which pilgrims made their way to the Vatican, the church made a tidy profit by charging for the crossing. Some of that toll money was spent on commissioning the statues of around a dozen angels that line the bridge as a sort of open-air sculpture museum – which gives the Aelian Bridge its modern name of the Ponte Sant'Angelo.

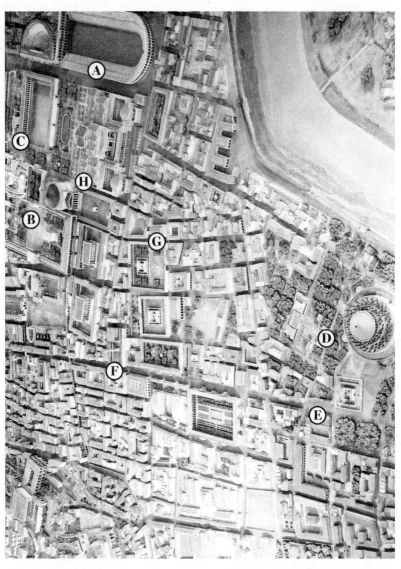

A STADIUM OF DOMITIAN

B SAEPTA JULIA

C BATHS OF AGRIPPA

D MAUSOLEUM OF AUGUSTUS

E ARA PACIS

F COLUMN OF AURELIUS

G COLUMN OF ANTONINUS

H PANTHEON

REGIO VII: THE CAMPUS MARTIUS

Urban Park and Playground

The Campus Martius was for many years an extensive open space on the north side of Rome. Roman legend claimed that these were the fields that belonged to Rome's last king, the tyrannical Tarquin the Proud. When Tarquin was unceremoniously ejected from Rome, his fields were dedicated to the Roman war god Mars. Those of a sceptical disposition might note that the Campus Martius was where the Roman levies once mustered for war, which were an annual event in the life of early Rome (Archaic Italy was a rough place).

The Field of Mars was also where young Romans regularly gathered for military training and exercises in horsemanship and there was from earliest times an already ancient altar to Mars at this location, although the altar itself has been gone for centuries. In other words, the name Campus Martius might not have got that name from the time of Tarquin but instead be what is known as a 'back formation'. Since the area already had that name, someone thought up a legend that explained it.

Because the census often coincided with the muster, which was a handy way of gathering all eligible male Romans citizens together in one place, for centuries the only building on the Campus Martius was the Villa Publica, where the censors did their work and stored their records.

Roma Al Fresco

Getting out of the city into the Campus Martius comes literally as a breath of fresh for the people of Rome.

The extent of the Campus is indeed remarkable. Chariot races and equestrian events can take place not only without interfering with each other but also yet leaving space for all the crowds who exercise by themselves by playing ball, rolling hoops or wrestling. Add the works of art situated around the Campus Martius and the ground covered with grass throughout the year. Then look at the hills with their tops looming above the river and then stretching down to the banks. The whole thing strikes the eye as a stage-painting. I'm telling you – it's a scene you can hardly look away from.

Strabo, *Geographia* (5.3.8)

The Baths of Agrippa

We begin by examining more closely the site of last night's bath. This took place in Rome's oldest public baths, the Baths of Agrippa. With the completion of the Aqua Virgo in 19 BC, Agrippa, who was at that time second in Rome only to Augustus, decided that he would use some of the water from this aqueduct to construct a novel kind of building, which the Romans of his day called the *sudatorium laconicum* or 'Spartan sweat lodge'. In theory, the design was based on the structures used by Spartan youths of old when they washed themselves down after their military exercises.

This building was revolutionary in another way. Until this point, there had been a tradition of leaving the Campus Martius clear of buildings to allow for military drills and the gathering of the Roman voting assembly called the *comitia centuriata*. Since the elections of the *comitia centuriata* were basically done by the Roman army in voting mode, this took up a lot of space. However, the need for a large open

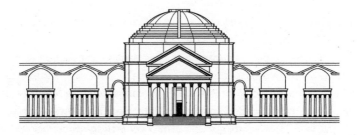

space was somewhat reduced, partly because the professional Roman army of the first century AD did not need to have an annual muster and because voting had been regularized by the construction of the Saepta Julia next to the baths (of which more shortly).

Agrippa's baths were relatively primitive compared with the spectacular efforts of later emperors, although they did establish the tradition of placing outstanding artwork within the grounds, including work by the great Lysippus, the favoured sculptor of Alexander the Great. However, Romans using these baths need not fear that their bathing experience will be a reversion to early Augustan austerity, because the baths were rebuilt on a more luxurious scale by Domitian after a fire in AD 80 and were recently remodelled again. The original baths lacked a *piscina*, probably because there was a swimming pool next door between the baths and the Tiber, this being the Stagnum Agrippae or 'Agrippa's pond', which was built not so much to indulge Romans bathers as to drain the rather swampy area and provide a more solid base for building (Augustus had plans of his own for the area).

The Saepta Julia

The name of this structure gives perhaps an inadvertent idea of what the Roman elite thought of Roman voters, although given the Roman penchant for irony, the name may originally have come from the voters themselves. *Saepta* means 'sheep pen'. Julius Caesar first conceived of the structure as a means of herding voters through the process as quickly and efficiently as possible, although the work was only completed after Caesar himself had fatally lost a vote of no confidence in the Roman senate.

Romans might also appreciate the irony in the fact that they voted for years in the wind and rain of the Campus Martius and finally got a properly built voting hall (in marble, no less) just at the moment when their votes became meaningless. These days the Saepta is used as a public space, often occupied by upmarket stalls, so one is more likely to encounter an aristocratic lady buying luxury goods than a politician buying votes, as happened in the good old days of the Republic.

It is still worth visiting the place though, and not just out of nostalgia for Rome's Republican past. There are two splendid murals on the porticos adjoining the building, one depicting Jason and the Argonauts and the other telling the story of the tragic Greek hero Meleager.

The Augustan Mausoleum

From here we detour northwards, pausing first at the Julio-Claudian *ustrinum*. Just as in times when inhumation is in fashion there is a family burial plot, when cremation is the norm many families have a family cremation site. This *ustrinum* is where the mortal remains of many of the Julio-Claudian clan were turned to ashes. There's a low wall running around the site with *cippi* placed in front of the wall (a *cippus*, you will recall, is a small marker post made of stone) and a fence protects the *cippi*. These markers give the names of most of the imperial family (from the time of Augustus) and all finish with the terse remark '*hic crematus est*' (cremated at this place). Trees are planted around the site, carefully spaced close enough to cover it with an appropriately sombre shade, but not so close as to add to the blaze when the *ustrinum* was in use.

Continue northwards until you reach the mausoleum itself. Augustus was a master of propaganda and saw no reason to stop carefully curating his image just because he was dead. Therefore, everything about Augustus' Mausoleum is a carefully constructed

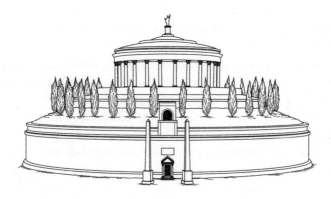

statement about the man himself and the posthumous image that he wanted to project.

Start with the location. As Strabo tells us in his *Geographia*, temples in this area are so ornate and clustered so closely that 'they seem to be trying to make the rest of the city a mere adjunct to this spot'. Strabo continues, 'Because this place is therefore considered to be the holiest of all, the Romans have placed here the tombs of their most illustrious men and women. The most noteworthy of these tombs is the Mausoleum ...' (Ibid.).

If you are worried about not finding the mausoleum amid this profusion of temples and tombs, don't be. There's no way you can miss it. In fact, it is one of the first things people see of Rome when they approach the city from the north, and it is visible from the moment you set foot in the Campus Martius. It is probable that Augustus had the Mausoleum at Halicarnassus in mind when he ordered the construction, because the dimensions (45 metres high and 100 metres in diameter) are close to those of that seventh wonder of the world. It is noteworthy that Hadrian, in constructing his own tomb, took care to come close but not to equal the overall area of Augustus' sepulchre.

Augustus intended his tomb to last and so it was built of sturdy tufa and concrete, even though these prosaic building materials are carefully shielded from the public gaze by acres of white marble and slabs of white travertine stone. As with Hadrian's tomb, the circular part of the mausoleum (the *tholos*) stands on a raised embankment – in this case planted with trees rather than statuary. Above that – and taking in about half the ground area of the overall site – is the dome of the *tholos* itself, topped off (as later became traditional) with a colossal statue of the tomb's main occupant.

Grave Intentions

The construction of Augustus' Mausoleum was a political act. At the time, Augustus (then Octavian) was locked in a struggle with Mark Antony for mastery of the empire. In a propaganda coup, Augustus had seized the last will and testament of Mark Antony from the Shrine of the Vestals where it had been deposited for safekeeping. He thereafter revealed that Antony wanted to be buried in Egypt, not in Rome. This was therefore the appropriate moment for Augustus to start building his own highly visible tomb to demonstrate that unlike the orientalizing Mark Antony, he, Augustus, was and would forever be a true Roman.

Entry to the tomb comes by way of a wide forecourt, which Augustus also adapted for propaganda purposes:

> *Augustus of sacred memory made remarkable use of the [obelisk] in the Campus Martius. He positioned it to mark the sun's shadow and thereby the hours of the day. The pavement was laid to length appropriating the height of the obelisk. At noon in midsummer the shadow cast by the obelisk reached exactly to the edge. Bronze rods set in the pavement were designed to measure the shadow daily as it gradually shortened and then lengthened again. A shiny golden ball was set atop the obelisk so that the tip of the shadow was given definition it would otherwise lack.*

> Pliny, *Natural History* (36.72–3)

Useful as it is, one notes that the shadow of the sundial falls parallel to the Via Flaminia that runs close by, and this direction draws the eye inevitably along the line of the shadow towards Augustus' tomb. It is probable that the shadow was designed to point directly towards the entrance, but this aspect of Augustan propaganda went awry within a generation. As Pliny reports:

> *For about the past thirty years readings from the sundial have not matched the calendar ... earth-tremors affecting the city may have caused a local displacement of the obelisk, or floods from the Tiber may have caused the mass to settle.*

Ibid.

That's the problem with building on a flood plain. Even though Pliny points out that Augustus caused the foundations to be dug to the same depth as the height of the structures they were to bear, the entrance to the tomb and the obelisk are both slowly sinking into the alluvial soil.

The *Res Gestae*

At the entrance to the Augustan Mausoleum – which is as far as most people are allowed to come – stand two bronze pillars bearing the text known as the *Res Gestae* (things achieved). This is literally Augustus attempting to have the last word – for the pillars list all that Augustus achieved in his lifetime, carefully eliding the bits he wanted posterity to forget and occasionally stretching half-truths to the point where they stop just short of being outright lies. Nevertheless, you cannot help feeling that you are standing at the monument to a truly remarkable man, whose legacy is not just this mausoleum, but the entire city and empire beyond.

Assuming you somehow get permission from the authorities, the interior of the tomb itself is approached through entrances in a series of support walls around the central structure. Passing through the fourth of these walls brings one to a narrow corridor that circles the base of the *tholos* before opening into the burial chamber itself. Here there are a series of alcoves containing the ashes of the imperial family members and a small square room set aside for the mortal remains of the divine Augustus himself.

Augustus suffered from poor health even when he was a child and was therefore rather startled to eventually discover that he had outlived most of his contemporaries – including his designated successors. These successors-who-weren't were all interred in the tomb before Augustus who was finally put to rest by his successor Tiberius, who was rather disgruntled that he had only got the job of emperor by virtue of being the last man standing.

> *After Augustus buried Agrippa in the tomb with you,*
>   *Marcellus,*
> *The same walls contained both of his sons-in-law,*
> *Then hardly had the doors slammed shut on Agrippa*
> *Than the sister of the emperor herself was given her funeral*
>   *rites.*
> *Three times lives have been taken, and now a fourth –*
> *For the tears of great Augustus are claimed by Drusus*
> *Fates! Close now the doors of a tomb used all too often*
> *Seal them shut, for they have been opened*
> *More than you should demand.*

> Ovid (attrib.), *Consolation to Livia* (67–74)

The Ara Pacis

From here turn down the flight of steps constructed for this purpose and proceed towards the Ara Pacis – the Altar of Peace. Peace was certainly the greatest of the accomplishments of Augustus. He came

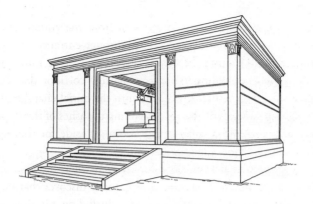

to power after almost a century of devastating civil strife, which had brought the Roman empire to its knees. By the time Augustus took control, people were less concerned with democracy and civil rights than that someone should somehow get the fighting to stop. The Ara Pacis was Augustus' declaration – literally set in stone – that this was what he had done and what he intended to keep doing.

Those used to the grandeur of some Roman monuments will be surprised by the modest size of the Ara Pacis – it's less than the size of a family dwelling. Yet size is not everything. The altar is venerated not only by lovers of peace but by those admirers of Roman sculpture at its finest. Almost the entire surface of the altar is taken up by a series of friezes beautifully carved in bas-relief that show figures that are at once idealized and startlingly lifelike.

The east and west panels show scenes from myth and figures such as Roma (the divine embodiment of the city) sitting surrounded by the bounty of a peaceful empire. Another scene shows the sacrifice of a pig, which was how the Romans of old had formally ratified a peace treaty. However, the most outstanding scene shows in stone the procession that was intended be re-enacted every year. Here come the lictors, the bodyguards and enforcers of the Roman magistrates who follow. Then the priests with one member of each of the sacred colleges represented on the frieze. Then come the women of the imperial family accompanied by their under-age children and some children in foreign dress. These latter represent the offspring of foreign powers who have sent their sons to Rome, the power that dominates the known world, partly as hostages and partly as guest-students of.

Another panel shows the entire imperial family of Augustus reverently proceeding to where a figure performs a sacrifice. Since Romans did nothing in the presence of the gods with their heads uncovered, it is hard to establish the identity of this veiled figure who may have been Augustus himself; after the progress of the centuries and the absence of any labels on the statues, it's difficult to work out who is who. That figure there, close to the veiled man – is it Livia, the wife of Augustus, or Julia, his later disgraced daughter? And which child is which? It's tricky to tell, but the message is unmistakable: here stands the family of Augustus, united with the leading officials of the empire, and the divine embodiments of the empire itself all dedicating themselves to the preservation of the Pax Romana (the Roman Peace). It's a powerful statement.

Continued on the Next Column ...

From here we move back towards the city, where another monument awaits our attention. This is yet another imperial funerary monument in the form of a fifteen-metre column dedicated to the Emperor Antoninus Pius (AD 138–61) and his wife Faustina. This column is in the style of that of Antoninus' predecessor but one, the Emperor Trajan, whose altogether more impressive column dominates his eponymous forum.

Trajan's Column is essentially a gigantic picture book telling the story of his Dacian war. In its own way, the Column of Antoninus is an equally impressive testament to his military achievements – which is to say, none. Under Antoninus, Rome delivered on the promise of the Ara Pacis: an empire prosperous and at peace. Millions of people, from the deserts of Syria to the bogs of Caledonia were quietly getting on with lives untroubled by barbarian invasions or civil strife. As his blank column testifies, Antoninus presided over one of mankind's most desirable states: life in uninteresting times.

The base of this statue is of white marble (you may have spotted a theme here) and the main panel shows Antoninus being escorted to the heavens by a deity who may be Aeon, the personification of eternity. On the other panels a cavalry escort seems to be watching the departure of the imperial couple.

While he would probably prefer it not to be the case, the successor to Antoninus, Marcus Aurelius (AD 161–80) had plenty to talk about on his column, which stands just south of his predecessor's, near the intersection of the Via Flaminia and the Via Recta. Marcus Aurelius was of a contemplative disposition; he has left as a legacy the longest text written by any Roman emperor, a book of stoic philosophy called the *Meditations*. Nevertheless, it was in the reign of Aurelius that Rome had first to face the fury of those Germanic invasions (in this particular case, the Marcomanni and the Sarmatians) that have troubled the empire ever since.

A competent if not particularly willing general, Aurelius successfully held off the invading enemy in a campaign that ran from AD 172 to AD 175. Taking his cue from Trajan, Aurelius had the story of his campaign carved on a spiral up a commemorative column in the Campus Martius. The imitation is explicit in that both columns are the same height – 30 metres – although Trajan's architect chose to taper the drums in his column, making them thinner towards the top. This produces an optical illusion that the column is taller than it actually is. Aurelius chose not to do this, so his column has a bulkier, more solid, look. Given the instability threatening his empire, this is probably the exact effect he was trying to achieve, for this column is in the end basically a propaganda statement.

Again, as with Trajan's, there is a spiral staircase within the column with strategically placed loopholes letting in light and air. A purist might contrast the realism and detail of Trajan's column with the somewhat cruder figures on the Aurelian column where the sculptors have instead stressed dynamism and action. There are also signs of a greater degree of Roman insecurity – Antoninus' column stresses the superiority of Roman arms and the leadership of the emperor, things airily taken for granted on the column of Trajan.

Just to the west of the column stands a temple dedicated to the memory of Marcus Aurelius by his son Commodus. In an outright refutation of the principle of hereditary abilities, while Marcus Aurelius is remembered as one of the best of Roman emperors, the disastrous Commodus easily ranks somewhere low in the bottom ten. Therefore, give Commodus' monument to his father a quick assessment as one of the few things that Commodus got right, then proceed westwards once more.

The next stop is to see the world – literally – from a long portico called the Porticus Vipsania. Agrippa, who was doing a lot of building in this area at the time, conceived of this portico as a means of honouring his sister, Vipsania. The structure is not only a useful site for sheltering from the elements, but also for browsing a map of the world as the Romans know it. Agrippa had already written a technical description of *orbis terra* (roughly 'planet earth') and now either he or Augustus ordered that this information be converted to visual form and chiselled into the marble wall of the portico as a map. As both Agrippa and his sister died before it was complete, it is known that Augustus – a relative by marriage – finished this family project.

The Pantheon

Before reaching the Pantheon – perhaps the most impressive temple in a city packed with impressive temples – stop and look to the north and imagine how Romans long ago must have felt about a now vanished architectural first that probably stood somewhere nearby. This is, or was, the Amphitheatre of Statilius Taurus. Amphitheatres in Rome were a relatively new phenomenon in the Late Republic, mainly because gladiatorial combat only then became more recognized as a spectator sport. There had been occasional gladiator combats over the previous century, but mainly staged as funeral games featuring relatively modest numbers of combatants.

However, once Roman politicians realized that the ordinary people (that is, ordinary voters) loved gladiator shows, they hastened to provide bigger and better venues for larger and bloodier exhibitions. Public gladiator shows were thereafter staged in temporary amphitheatres, although rickety construction and an overload of spectators on occasion made taking a seat in the stands as dangerous as participating in events in the arena below. After yet another lethal amphitheatre collapse, Statilius Taurus, a successful general of Augustus, built a solid, permanent amphitheatre somewhere here on the Campus Martius. This structure proved somewhat less permanent than he had hoped, as an earth tremor and a fire put paid to the structure within a few decades – but by then this amphitheatre had been eclipsed in any case by the bigger, better and more central Flavian Amphitheatre at the Colosseum.

And so to the Pantheon. The name says that the temple is dedicated to all (*pan*) gods (*theon*), which actually means to all the gods of the official Roman religion. In fact, though, this is a temple celebrating that wonder of Roman building material: concrete.

Roman concrete is the best in the world. Certainly, it is better than any that will be produced over the next 2,000 years. So good is it that, with very old buildings where poorly fired bricks have

Superior Cement

There are several reasons for the extraordinary strength of Roman concrete. The first is that the aggregate added to the cement is particularly solid (Roman concrete is laid rather than poured). Secondly, Roman concrete is hydraulic, which means that the wetter it gets, the harder it sets. Finally, the Romans use *pulvis puteolanus*: fine soil from volcanic beds originally from around Naples, but also from deposits near Rome. There's something about this soil, when added to cement, that reacts when water seeps into the fine cracks that any concrete develops over time. This combination of water and elements within the soil creates a new compound, which forms within the crack and effectively seals it, making Roman concrete to some extent self-healing.

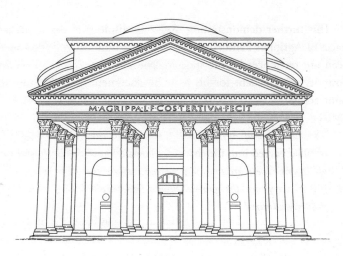

eroded or melted away, the concrete that once held the bricks in place remains as a delicate lattice of mortar.

If one is going to build the largest free-standing concrete dome in the world, ever, then Roman concrete is what that dome should be built of. Yet when the Pantheon was originally built under the orders of Marcus Agrippa, this dome did not exist. Agrippa's temple, in fact, was a relatively modest affair. In his day, the western part of the Campus Martius had not yet been given over to extensive building projects, and the imperial government was taking the first tentative steps to see how the public felt about this.

Public disapproval of Agrippa's temple was more than somewhat mollified by the great popularity of Agrippa's baths, as the Roman people realized that they could not disapprove of building on the Campus Martius in the one case but not in the other. It also helped that Agrippa was building not on the publicly owned part of the campus but on property he owned already. Evidently the gods were harder to please than the Roman public because the temple was destroyed by fire in AD 80. Unable to take the hint, the Emperor Domitian rebuilt it again only for the place to burn down once more in AD 110, this time after a lightning strike.

This further demonstration of divine displeasure has erased all traces of Agrippa's Pantheon. The only indications of what had once been are references by the indefatigable Pliny the Elder to whom posterity owes a debt for his habit of documenting everything he came across:

> *The Pantheon of Agrippa is decorated with caryatids* [a type of pillar carved into the shape of a female figure] *by Diogenes of Athens. These are top-quality pieces, as are the other groups* [of statuary] *on the gables, though these are too high to be properly admired.*
>
> Pliny the Elder, *Natural History* (36.38)

We know also from the writer Cassius Dio (*History* [53.27]) that Agrippa wanted to put a statue of his emperor and patron, Augustus, within the temple. Augustus refused permission (probably because the other statues were to Rome's gods, among whom is Nemesis, the goddess who punishes excessive pride). Agrippa instead set up the statue immediately in front of his Pantheon. He still slipped in an extra bit of flattery though: because Venus was a prominent Roman deity, she naturally had a place within the Pantheon, but her statue was afforded special honour because Venus was traditionally the founder of Rome's Julian line, to which Augustus belonged.

It fell to that most enthusiastic of builders, the Emperor Hadrian, to reconstruct the Pantheon in the form it has today, including that epic concrete dome that makes it so different from all other Roman temples. Hadrian modestly did not put his name to the new temple, but instead added an inscription – ostensibly a copy of the original – crediting the building to Marcus Agrippa. As this act of exemplary modesty is mentioned in every text about the Pantheon, it appears that Hadrian did a magnificent job of promoting his name and image by not doing so.

The reconstructed Pantheon faces north (the original probably faced south), with a forecourt made of slabs of granite. Within, the floor is of porphyry and coloured marble. Niches run along the walls containing shrines to all gods great and small. The real eye-catcher, though, is the ceiling, that great overarching concrete dome, gilded golden and topped off by an opening (the *oculus*) 9 metres in diameter through which solid beams of sunlight illuminate the temple interior. The height from the *oculus* to the floor is 43.2 metres. This is exactly the same as the inner diameter of the temple. In other words, if you extrapolated the dome to a complete sphere, you would fill in the inner space almost completely, with the lowest point of the sphere hovering less than a hand's breadth from the floor. (And even that distance is probably due to settling of the temple's foundations rather than an imperfection in the original design.)

While the dome is visible for miles, very little of the rest of the back and sides of the temple is visible because of the public buildings surrounding it. Hadrian was so proud of his restored temple that he would regularly hold court for clients and petitioners, sometimes seated before the huge bronze doors that open on to the *pronaos* (basically the temple's front porch). Here there are three rows of Corinthian columns. The front ones are of grey granite and those in shadow at the back are made of lighter stone, giving the *pronaos* a pleasingly even appearance.

On the very front, the bold inscription reads: 'M. AGRIPPA L.F. COS TERTIUM FECIT', Romans accustomed to the terse style of inscriptional Latin have no trouble expanding this to *Marcus Agrippa, Lucius Filius, Consul Tertium, Fecit*. That is: 'Marcus Agrippa, the son of Lucius, three times consul, made this.'

Vale Roma

It is time now to make your way northwards along the Flaminian Way. As you get to the north-west portion of the Pincian Hill, just before the Porta Flaminia, stop at the family tomb of the Domitii, one of the ancient aristocratic families of Rome. Look for a balustrade of marble from the Greek island of Thasos and a marble altar beyond that. There you will see a sarcophagus containing the mortal remains of the Emperor Nero. As with most things connected with this murderous despot, the whole thing is in excellent taste.

All that remains is to make your way against the flow of traffic coming through the Porta Flaminia. This is no easy task as much of the world seems determined to press its way into Rome for which reason this gate is designed more with a view to traffic control than defence.

Proceed up the Via Flaminia towards Falerii and let the clamour of the bustling city fade behind you. Down this road in future years will come barbarian invaders, the unwitting bearers of devastating plagues and almost as destructive, the armies of the Eastern Roman Empire trying to reclaim Rome as their own. The city will be battered by enemies and mauled by civil strife. Many of its ancient monuments will be destroyed even as their legend lives on. And Rome, the Eternal City, will survive.

THE TWENTY-FIRST CENTURY WALK

Since medieval times, the grass of the Campus Martius has been comprehensively paved over and the area is thoroughly urbanized. One of the most recognized features today is at the roads that lead to the junction of the Acqua Vergine aqueduct, ancient Rome's Aqua Virgo. These three roads (*tri viae*) end at the world-famous Trevi fountain, a gorgeous monument to baroque excess. Although built by the popes, one of the main figures is the pagan god Oceanus and his accompanying Tritons. Another nod to antiquity is a statuary group showing Agrippa commanding his subordinates to build the aqueduct.

Of actual antiquity there is less to see. The ruins of the Baths of Agrippa survived until some time in the 1500s, probably because the building was too much effort to mine for stone when there were so many other exploitable buildings available. Today only a forlorn section of wall remains from the central part of the baths.

The Mausoleum of Augustus is also still there, and in better shape than it has been for centuries thanks to extensive repair work. The ashes of the imperial family, including those of Augustus, appear to have been scattered into the winds while the structure itself has led a series of strange afterlives. In the twelfth century the building was a fortress belonging to one of Rome's noble families, and as times became more peaceful the collapsed top was changed into a sort of hanging gardens adorned with salvaged Roman statuary.

In the eighteenth century the mausoleum passed into the hands of a Portuguese aristocrat who staged bullfights there. When the city of Rome finally reclaimed ownership of the mausoleum in 1908, a stage was built on the old cylindrical base and under the name of the Auditorium Augusteo. The final resting place of Augustus became a famous concert venue.

The auditorium lasted until Rome's next would-be emperor, Mussolini, decided to restore the building as an imperial tomb. He personally took the first swing with a sledgehammer that cleared away all the accoutrements that the tomb had collected over the centuries and attempted to restore the tomb to its original imperial condition. While he was at it, Mussolini ordered the demolition of the buildings that surrounded the tomb to create today's plaza, the Piazza Augusto Imperatore.

With the fall of Mussolini, the tomb of Augustus was again abandoned to litter, graffiti and weeds to the extent that it became something of a scandal. Only very recently, after previous plans failed due to lack of funds, has a major restoration project finally got off the ground. In keeping with the usual Italian approach to restoring monuments, this may take considerably longer than it took to build the thing in the first place – but the final result should be well worth the wait.

The Ara Pacis is another Augustan monument that owes its current form to Mussolini. In previous centuries the magnificent artwork of the altar had proven its undoing and art lovers had dismantled almost the entire structure and redistributed it among the noble houses of Rome and museums around Europe. Even today the Italian authorities are still battling various museums for the original pieces, but enough were returned to allow Mussolini to rebuild the structure, though not quite in its original location.

The original building that housed the altar proved unsatisfactory, and in 2006 a firm of architects came up with the current design: an airy glass-walled structure with views of the Tiber. Despite its new location, the Ara Pacis has not yet been able to shake the taint of its association with the fascist regime of Mussolini and is still the target of occasional ideological vandalism.

While the column of Antoninus Pius has vanished into history (and the base into a Vatican museum), the column of Marcus Aurelius is still standing, although Marcus Aurelius has been displaced from the top by a statue of St Paul. The reliefs on the base were lost when the column was renovated by Pope Sixtus V in 1589, and an inscription added wrongly claiming that this is the Antonine column (the mistake was only discovered in the eighteenth century).

The column now stands proudly in its own public square, only slightly the worse for wear after its passage through the centuries. One of the best ways to view this column is to seek out an upstairs coffee shop in one of the buildings surrounding the piazza and from here examine the building and wonder what Marcus Aurelius would think of his monument in its modern surroundings.

The Pantheon survived the destruction of many Roman monuments by converting to Christianity, and was for generations known as The Church of Saint Mary and the Martyrs. The building did lose some of its bronze and marble (some bits are now, for example, in the British Museum), but it is by far the best preserved of all the ancient temples in Rome. The massive bronze doors have somehow escaped predation through the ages and remain where Hadrian's builders installed them.

Pope Urban added a pair of bell towers, which Romans mockingly called 'the donkey's ears', and these were removed around the time that the building passed into the care of Italy's Ministry of Cultural Heritage and Activities and Tourism. Visitors are reminded that the building is still a Catholic church and visitors are expected to show proper decorum while within.

Getting within can take up to twenty minutes of waiting in line at busy times, so viewing this building is best done at quiet times at the end of the day (as a church the Pantheon is open late and entry is free). Thereafter one can enjoy dinner in one of the many trattorias nearby.

SOURCES

Ammianus Marcellinus, *History*
Apicius, *On the Subject of Cooking*
Apuleius, *The Golden Ass*
Cassius Dio, *History*
Corpus Inscriptionum Latinarum (CIL)
Dionysius of Halicarnassus, *Roman Antiquities*
Herodian, *Roman History*
Horace, *Satires*
Juvenal, *Satires*
Livy, *Ab Urbe Condida*
Martial, *Epigrams*
Martial, *Satires*
Ovid (attrib.), *Consolation to Livia*
Ovid, *Fasti*
Pliny the Elder, *Natural History*
Plutarch, *Life of C. Gracchus*
Plutarch, *Life of Romulus*
Plutarch, *Roman Questions*
Quintilian, *On Oratory*
Statius, *Silvae*
Strabo, *Geographia*
Suetonius, *Life of Augustus*
Suetonius, *Life of Nero*
Suetonius, *Life of Vespasian*
Tacitus, *Annals*
Valerius Maximus, *The Deeds and Sayings of Famous Men*
Victor, *De Caesaribus: Marcus Aurelius*
Vitruvius, *De Architectura*

INDEX